THE BORROWER IS RESPONSIBLE
FOR RETURNING THIS BOOK ON
THE DATE SHOWN ABOVE.

CLEARWATER CAMPUS LIBRARY

S P J C

PORTRAITS OF WOMEN

Lady Mary Wortley Montagu

PORTRAITS OF WOMEN

BY

GAMALIEL BRADFORD

With Illustrations

Essay Index Reprint Series

 BOOKS FOR LIBRARIES PRESS
FREEPORT, NEW YORK

First Published 1916
Reprinted 1969

STANDARD BOOK NUMBER:
8369-1247-0

LIBRARY OF CONGRESS CATALOG CARD NUMBER:
75-90611

PRINTED IN THE UNITED STATES OF AMERICA

TO
MY DAUGHTER

Out, hyperbolical fiend! talkest thou nothing but of ladies?

TWELFTH NIGHT.

PREFACE

THE nine portraits contained in this volume are preliminary studies or sketches for the series of portraits of American women which will follow my Union portraits. Such a collection of portraits of women will certainly fill a most important section in the gallery of historical likenesses selected from the whole of American history, which it is my wish to complete, if possible.

There is always a certain impertinence about a man's attempt to portray the characters of women. And this impertinence is not got rid of by the charming, but not wholly felicitous, epigraph of Sainte-Beuve's *Portraits de Femmes:* "*Avez vous donc été femme, Monsieur, pour prétendre ainsi nous connâitre?*"—"*Non, Madame, je ne suis pas le devin Tirésias, je ne suis qu'un humble mortel qui vous a beaucoup aimées.*" There is, however, an equal impertinence in trying to portray the characters of men, indeed of anybody but one's self, and though this last undertaking is always delightful, it is apt to lead to even more astonishing results than accompany one's attempts upon others. While endeavoring constantly to strengthen and deepen the accuracy of my portraits as regards mere fact, I yet become more and more convinced that their value must be more in suggestion and stimulation than in any reliable or final presentment of character. Such presentments do not exist.

PREFACE

The selection of portraits in this volume has grown in a rather haphazard way. Although the types depicted differ from one another, sometimes with marked contrast, still, if I had planned the series deliberately as a whole, I should have picked out figures more representative of entirely different lines of life. A disadvantage, much more marked in portraying women than in portraying men, is the necessity of dealing with exceptions rather than with average personages. The psychographer must have abundant material, and usually it is women who have lived exceptional lives that leave such material behind them. The psychography of queens and artists and authors and saints is little, if any, more interesting, than that of your mother or mine, or of the first shopgirl we meet. I would paint the shopgirl's portrait with the greatest pleasure, but the material is lacking.

It will be noted, also, that none of these portraits presents the modern woman. Eugénie de Guérin is the latest in date and she is about as modern as Eve. The projection of woman into the very middle of the stage of active life, her participation on equal terms in almost all the lines of man's achievement, are effecting the vastest social revolution since the appearance of Christianity. The outcome of this revolution is something no man — or woman — can foresee. But its most obvious and perhaps principal effect is in moulding the life, character, and habits of man. Woman already dominates our manners, our morals, our literature, our stage, our private finances. She proposes to dominate our politics. And it is by no means sure that she will not end by the subjugation of our intelligence. This feminine supremacy obtains, if I am correctly informed, in the kingdom of the spiders and also, according to some seers, in the most advanced development of the planetary worlds. While such a conquest must, of course, to some extent, react upon the conqueror, it seems probable that the fundamental instincts of the feminine temperament are what they were a thousand, or two thousand years ago, and that the new woman remains the same old woman in a little different garb, which propensity to a little different garb is the oldest thing about her.

As I have already explained in the preface to "Union Portraits," the word "Portrait" is very unsatisfactory, in spite of the high authority of Sainte-Beuve. Analogies between different arts are always misleading and this particular analogy is particularly objectionable. Critics, otherwise kindly, have urged that a portrait takes a man only at one special moment of his life and may therefore be quite untrue to the larger lines of his character. This is perfectly just, and the word "psychographs" should be substituted for "portraits." Psychography aims at precisely the opposite of photography. It seeks to extricate from the fleeting, shifting, many-colored tissue of a man's long life those habits of action, usually known as qualities of character, which are the slow product of inheritance and training, and which, once formed at a comparatively early age, usually alter little and that only by imperceptible degrees. The art of psychography is to disentangle these habits from the immaterial, inessential matter of biography,

PREFACE

to illustrate them by touches of speech and action that
are significant and by those only, and thus to burn
them into the attention of the reader, not by any
means as a final or unchangeable verdict, but as something that cannot be changed without vigorous thinking on the part of the reader himself.

But "Psychographs of Women," on the back of a
book, is as yet rather startling for the publisher, for
the purchaser, and even for me.

GAMALIEL BRADFORD

WELLESLEY HILLS, MASS.
May 26, 1916

CONTENTS

ILLUSTRATIONS

PORTRAITS OF WOMEN

I

LADY MARY WORTLEY MONTAGU

CHRONOLOGY

Lady Mary Pierrepont.
Born London, May 26, 1689.
Married Edward Wortley Montagu,
   August 16, 1712.
In Constantinople 1716–1718.
In Italy 1739–1761.
Husband died 1761.
Died London, August 21, 1762.

PORTRAITS OF WOMEN

I

LADY MARY WORTLEY MONTAGU

LADY MARY WORTLEY MONTAGU (born Pierrepont) wrote poems, essays, and translations of some note in her own day, of none in ours. She also wrote letters which can never die, letters less charming, indeed, than Madame de Sévigné's because the writer was less charming, but full of light for the first half of the eighteenth century and also for Lady Mary herself. I do not refer so much to the celebrated letters from Constantinople, because those were probably arranged and edited for literary purposes, but to the general correspondence, which throbs and vibrates and sparkles like a live thing.

The writer knew quite well what she was doing. Speaking of Madame de Sévigné's productions she says: "Mine will be full as entertaining forty years hence." And, perhaps with a touch of jealousy not wholly uncharacteristic, she depreciates her French predecessor, "who only gives us, in a lively manner and fashionable phrases, mean sentiments, vulgar prejudices, and endless repetitions. Sometimes the tittle-tattle of a fine lady, sometimes the tittle-tattle of an old nurse, always tittle-tattle." Those who find the divine tittle-tattle of "Notre Dame des Rochers" not only among the liveliest, but among the most human and even the wisest, things in literature, will not be the less ready to appreciate Lady Mary, who has her own tittle-tattle as well as her own wisdom and liveliness. How easy she is, how ready, and how graceful. Her letters, she says, are "written with rapidity and sent without reading over." This may be true and may not. At any rate, they have, at their best, the freshness of first thoughts, the careless brilliancy of a high-bred, keen-witted woman, talking in her own parlor, indifferent to effect, yet naturally elegant, in her speech, as in her dress and motion.

With what vivacity she touches everything and everybody about her, "a certain sprightly folly that (I thank God) I was born with" she calls it, but it is only folly in the sense of making dull things gay and sad things tolerable. See how she finds laughter in the imminence of sea peril. An ancient English lady "had bought a fine point head, which she was contriving to conceal from the custom-house officers. . . . When the wind grew high, and our little vessel cracked, she fell heartily to her prayers, and thought wholly of her soul. When it seemed to abate, she returned to the worldly care of her head-dress, and addressed herself to me: 'Dear madam, will you take care of this point? If it should be lost! — Ah, Lord, we shall all be lost! — Lord have mercy on my soul! — Pray, madam, take care of this head-dress.' This easy transition from her soul to her head-dress, and the alternate agonies that both gave her, made it hard to determine which she thought of greatest value."

In the constant imminence of life's world perils Lady

LADY MARY WORTLEY MONTAGU

Mary had still by her this resource of merriment, which some call flippancy, but which, by any name, is not without its comforts.

True, such a glib tongue or pen is a dangerous plaything and liable to abuse. Lady Mary's own daughter said that her mother was too apt to set down people of a meek and gentle character for fools. People of any character, perhaps, whenever the wayward fancy struck her. She darted her shafts right and left. They stung and they clung, for they were barbed, if not poisoned. Sometimes they made near friends as cold as strangers. Too often they turned indifferent strangers into enemies. Enemies, too many, Lady Mary had all her life, and they seized on her weak points and amplified or invented ugly things about her till those who admire her most find defence somewhat difficult.

Yet she did not gloat over evil. "'T is always a mortification to me to observe there is no perfection in humanity." Her unkindness was far more on her tongue than in her heart. "This I know, that revenge has so few joys for me, I shall never lose so much time as to undertake it." She had the keenest sense of human sorrow and suffering: "I think nothing so terrible as objects of misery, except one had the God-like attribute of being able to redress them." What she could do to redress them she did. In her efforts to introduce inoculation for smallpox she surely proved herself one of the greatest benefactors of humanity. In many smaller things, also, she was kindly and sympathetic. And what pleases me most is that she makes little mention of such deeds herself. One is left to divine them from curt, half-sarcastic remarks in other connections. Thus, during her long residence in Italy, it appears that she ministered to her neighbors both in body and soul. "I do what good I am able in the village round me, which is a very large one; and have had so much success, that I am thought a great physician, and should be esteemed a saint if I went to mass." Later she had much ado to keep the people from erecting a statue to her. But she shrank from love in Italy which was sure to breed laughter in England.

Also, even in her bursts of ill-nature, she had a certain reserve, a certain control, a certain sobriety. Indeed, she compliments herself, in old age, on her freedom from petulance. "To say truth, I think myself an uncommon kind of creature, being an old woman without superstition, peevishness, or censoriousness." This is, perhaps, more than we could say for her. But in youth and age both she loved moderation and shunned excess. When she was twenty-three, she wrote, "I would throw off all partiality and passion, and be calm in my opinion." She threw them off too much, she was too calm, she was cold. Walpole called her letters too womanish, but Lady Craven thought they must have been written by a man. Most readers will agree with Lady Craven. Even her vivacity lacks warmth. And it is here that she most falls short of the golden sunshine of Madame de Sévigné. Lady Mary is not quite the woman, even in her malice. Through her wit, through her thought, through her comment on life, even through her human relations runs a strain of something that was masculine.

LADY MARY WORTLEY MONTAGU

Nowhere is this more curious and amusing than in her love and marriage. She was beautiful, and knew it, though the smallpox, by depriving her of eyelashes, had given a certain staring boldness to her eyes. When she was over thirty, she "led up a ball" and "believed in her conscience she made one of the best figures there." When she was old, for all her philosophy, she did not look in a glass for eleven years. "The last reflexion I saw there was so disagreeable, I resolved to spare myself such mortifications for the future."

She fed her youthful fancy with the vast fictions then in fashion and the result was a romantic head and a cool heart. These appear alternately in her strange correspondence with her lover and future husband, Edward Wortley Montagu. When they first met, the gentleman admired her learning — at fourteen! And Latinity seems to have drawn them together quite as much as love. There was a sister, Miss Anne Wortley, and sisters are of great use on such occasions. Lady Mary wrote to her in language of extravagant regard, and Miss Wortley wrote back — at her brother's dictation. Then it became obviously simpler for the lovers to write direct.

Obstacles arose. Mr. Wortley Montagu would make no settlement on his wife. Lady Mary's father would not hear of a marriage without one, and hunted up another suitor, rich — and unacceptable. There was doubt, debate, delay — and then an elopement. Lady Mary eloping! What elements of comedy! And her letters make it so.

That she loved her lover as much as she could love is

evident. "My protestations of friendship are not like other people's, I never speak but what I mean, and when I say I love, 't is for ever." "I am willing to abandon all conversation but yours. If you please I will never see another man. In short, I will part with anything for you, but you. I will not have you a month to lose you for the rest of my life." "I would die to be secure of your heart, though but for a moment."

Yet this apparent passion is tempered with doubt and reversal. She cannot make him happy, nor he her. "I can esteem, I can be a friend, but I don't know whether I can love." "You would be soon tired with seeing every day the same thing." No, it is all folly. Cancel it, break it up, throw it over. Begin again, a new life, a new world. She will write to him no more. "I resolve against all correspondence of the kind; my resolutions are seldom made, and never broken."

This one is broken in a few days. Again she loves, again she hopes. Everything shall be right, so far as it lies with her. "If my opinion could sway, nothing should displease you. Nobody ever was so disinterested as I am." And yet once more cold analysis twitches her sleeve, murmurs in her ear. "You are the first I ever had a correspondence with, and I thank God I have done with it for all my life." "When I have no more to say to you, you will like me no longer."

Then she blows the doubts away, makes her stolen marriage, gives all to love, and in the very doing of it, lets fall one word that shows the doubter more than ever (italics mine): "I foresee all that will happen on

8

this occasion. I shall incense my family in the highest degree. The generality of the world will blame my conduct . . .; yet, '*t is possible*, you may recompence everything to me." How two little words will show a heart!

And afterwards? She fared pretty much as she expected. Love hardened into marriage with some, not unusual, hours of agony. "I cannot forbear any longer telling you, I think you use me very unkindly." When he fails to write to her, she cries for two hours. Then all becomes domestic, and decorous, and as it should be; and her matured opinion of marriage agrees very well with the previsions of her youth. "Where are people matched? I suppose we shall all come right in Heaven; as in a country dance, the hands are strangely given and taken, while they are in motion, at last all meet their partners when the jig is done."

Perhaps because she showed no great conjugal affection, there was plenty of gossip about affection less legitimate. Pope lavished rhetorical devotion on her. She laughed at it and, I fear, at him. In consequence he lampooned her with the savage spite of an eighteenth-century poet. She said unkind things about Sir Robert Walpole and Sir Robert's son said unkind things about her, mentioned some lovers by name, and implied many others. Lady Mary's careful editors have dealt with these slanders most painstakingly; and though in one case, that of an Italian adventure, they have overlooked a passage in Sir Horace Mann's letters oddly confirmatory of Walpole, I think they have cleared their heroine with entire success.

After all, Lady Mary's best defense against scandal is her own temperament and her own words. It is true, those who have lived a wild life are often the first to exclaim against it. But in this case the language bears every mark of being prompted by observation rather than experience. She says of the notorious Lady Vane: "I think there is no rational creature that would not prefer the life of the strictest Carmelite to the round of hurry and misfortune she has gone through."

Lady Mary's long sojourn in Italy towards the close of her life did much to increase suspicion in regard to her relations with her husband. Her greatest admirers have not been able to explain clearly why she wished to exile herself in such a fashion. But the tone in which, during the whole period, she writes both to Mr. Wortley Montagu and of him, is absolutely incompatible with any serious coldness between them. "My most fervent wishes are for your health and happiness." And again: "I have never heard from her since, nor from any other person in England, which gives me the greatest uneasiness; but the most sensible part of it is in regard of your health, which is truly and sincerely the dearest concern I have in this world."

Lady Mary had two children, and as a mother she is very much what she is as a wife, reasonable, prudent, devoted, but neither clinging nor adoring. She had, indeed, a happy art of expressing maternal tenderness, as of expressing everything, by which I do not imply that her feelings were not sincere, but simply that they were not very vital or very overwhelming. When she sets out on her travels, she is heartbroken over the perils and exposures for her son: "I have long learnt to hold myself at nothing; but when I think of the fatigue my poor infant must suffer, I have all a mother's fondness in my eyes, and all her tender passions in my heart." But her language about this same son, when grown to manhood, is somewhat astounding. He was a most extraordinary black sheep, wasted money, contracted debts, gambled, liked evil occupations and worse company, varied a multiplicity of wives with a multiplicity of religions, was once in jail, and never respectable. All this Lady Mary deplores, but she is not driven to despair by it; on the contrary, she analyzes his character to his father with singular cold soberness. "It is very disagreeable to me to converse with one from whom I do not expect to hear a word of truth, and, who, I am very sure, will repeat many things that never passed in our conversation." Or, more generally, "I suppose you are now convinced I have never been mistaken in his character; which remains unchanged, and what is yet worse, I think is unchangeable. I never saw such a complication of folly and falsity as in his letter to Mr. G."

Her daughter, Lady Bute, she was fond of. "Your happiness," she writes to her, "was my first wish, and the pursuit of all my actions, divested of all self-interest." Nevertheless, she lived contentedly without seeing her for twenty years.

That Lady Mary was a good manager domestically hardly admits of doubt; but I find no evidence that she loved peculiarly feminine occupations, though she does somewhere remark that she considers certain types of learned ladies "much inferior to the plain sense of a cook maid, who can make a good pudding and keep the kitchen in good order." Among her numerous benefactions in Italy was the teaching of her neighbors how to make bread and butter.

It is said that her servants loved her, not unnaturally, if she carried out her own maxim: "The small proportion of authority that has fallen to my share (only over a few children and servants) has always been a burden, . . . and I believe every one finds it so who acts from a maxim . . . that whoever is under my power is under my protection." She was a natural aristocrat, however, both socially and politically, and any leveling tendencies that she may have cherished in the ardor of youth, vanished entirely with years and experience. "Was it possible for me to elevate anybody from the station in which they were born, I now would not do it: perhaps it is a rebellion against that Providence that has placed them; all we ought to do is to endeavour to make them easy in the rank assigned them." And elsewhere, in a much more elaborate passage, she expresses herself with a deliberate haughtiness of rank and privilege which has rarely been surpassed. In her youth, she says, silly prejudice taught her that she was to treat no one as an inferior. But she has learned better and come to see that such a notion made her "admit many familiar acquaintances, of which I have heartily repented every one, and the greatest examples I have known of honor and integrity have been among those of the highest birth and fortunes." The English tendency to mingle classes and level dis-

tinctions will, she believes, have some day fatal con-
sequences. How curious, in so keen a wit, the failure
to foresee that just this English social elasticity would
avert the terrible disaster which was to befall the neat
gradations of French order and system!

Lady Mary was not only practical in her household,
but in all the other common concerns of life. Few
women have pushed their husbands on in the world
with more vigorous energy than is shown in the letters
she writes to Mr. Wortley Montagu, urging him to
drop his diffidence and claim what he deserves. "No
modest man ever did, or ever will, make his fortune."

As regards money, also, she was eminently a woman
of business — too eminently, say her enemies. One
reason alleged for her quarrel with Pope is his well-
meant advice which brought her large losses in South
Sea speculation. However much one may like and
admire her, it is impossible wholly to explain away
Walpole's picture of her sordid avarice, which cannot
be omitted, though hideous. "Lady Mary Wortley is
arrived; I have seen her; I think her avarice, her dirt,
and her vivacity are all increased. Her dress, like her
languages, is a *galimatias* of several countries, the
groundwork, rags; and the embroidery nastiness. She
wears no cap, no handkerchief, no gown, no petticoat,
no shoes. An old black-laced hood represents the first;
the fur of a horseman's coat, which replaces the third,
serves for the second; a dimity petticoat is deputy, and
officiates for the fourth; and slippers act the part of the
last."

It is easy to see here the brush of hatred deepening

the colors; but hatred can hardly have invented the whole. Yet all the references to money matters in Lady Mary's letters are sane and commendable. She hates poverty, and she hates extravagance as the road to poverty, and she cherishes thrift as the assurance of independence and comfort. That sort of lavish living which is certain to end in suffering for self and others she condemns bitterly. Will any one say she can condemn it too bitterly? "He lives upon rapine — I mean running in debt to poor people, who perhaps he will never be able to pay." But I do not find that she cherishes money for itself. We should seek riches, she says, but why? "As the world is, and will be, 't is a sort of duty to be rich, that it may be in one's power to do good, riches being another word for power." With which compare the remark of Gray, a man surely not liable to the charge of avarice: "It is a striking thing that one can't only not live as one pleases, but where and with whom one pleases, without money. Swift somewhere says, that money is liberty; and I fear money is friendship, too, and society, and almost every external blessing. It is a great, though ill-natured, comfort, to see most of those who have it in plenty, without pleasure, without liberty, and without friends."

Nevertheless, it must be admitted that in these questions of conduct Lady Mary does not err on the side of enthusiasm. In a long and curious passage she enlarges on the virtues of her favorite model — Atticus, the typical trimmer and opportunist, who lived in one of the greatest crises of the world, and weathered it safe and rich, who had many friends and served many and betrayed none, but did not think any cause good enough to die for.

As regards social life and general human relations, it is very much the same. Lady Mary had vast acquaintance. I do not find that she had many friends, either dear or intimate. Of Lady Oxford she does, indeed, always speak with deep affection. And she says of herself, no doubt truly: "I have a constancy in my nature that makes me always remember my old friends." Also her love of a snapping exchange of wit made her appreciate conversation. "You know I have ever been of opinion that a chosen conversation composed of a few that one esteems is the greatest happiness of life." Yet she was too full of resources to need people, too critical to love people, too little sympathetic to pity people. And in one of the lightning sentences of self-revelation she shows a temperament not perfectly endowed by heaven for friendship: "I manage my friends with such a strong yet with a gentle hand, that they are both willing to do whatever I have a mind to."

But, if she did not love mankind, she found them endlessly amusing, a perpetual food for observation and curiosity. And the wandering life she led nourished this taste to the fullest degree. "It was a violent transition from your palace and company to be locked up all day with my chambermaid, and sleep at night in a hovel; but my whole life has been in the Pindaric style." It is this love of diversity, this keen sense of the human in all its phases, which give zest to her Turkish letters and the record of wanderings and hardships which might not now be encountered in a journey to the Pole. But long wanderings and strange faces are not necessary for the naturalist of souls who can find the ugliest weeds and tenderest flowers at his own front door. Lady Mary was never tired of studying souls and thought highly of her own discernment in them. "I have seldom been mistaken in my first judgment of those I thought it worth while to consider." This confidence I am sorry to find in her; for I have always believed it a good rule that those who asserted their sure judgment of men knew little about them. True insight is more modest. At any rate, mistaken or not, she found the varied spectacle of human action end-lessly diverting and again and again recurs to the charm of it: "I endeavour upon this occasion to do as I have hitherto done in all the odd turns of my life; turn them, if I can, to my diversion." "I own I enjoy vast delight in the folly of mankind; and, God be praised, that is an inexhaustible source of entertainment."

Thus she could always amuse herself with men and women. At the same time, she could amuse herself without them and needed neither courtship nor cards nor gossip to keep her heart at ease. It is true that in youth she knew youth's restlessness, and that haunting dread, chronic to some souls, which fills one day with anxiety as to what may fill the next. To Mrs. Hewet she writes: "Be so good as never to read a letter of mine but in one of those minutes when you are entirely alone, weary of everything, and *inquiète* to think of what you shall do next. All people who live in the country must have some of those minutes." But time

soothes this and makes the present seem so insufficient
that the poor shreds of life remaining can never quite
eke it out. "I have now lived almost seven years in a
stricter retirement than yours in the Isle of Bute, and
can assure you, I have never had half an hour heavy on
my hands, for want of something to do."

Her country life did not, indeed, include much ecstasy over the natural world. She was born too early
for Rousseau and it is doubtful whether high romance
could ever have seriously appealed to her. She finds
Venice a gay social centre. Of its poetry, its mystery,
its moonlight, never a word. Perhaps these did not
exist before Byron. On the Alps and their sublimity
she has as delightful a phrase as the whole eighteenth
century can furnish (italics mine): "The prodigious
prospect of mountains covered with eternal snow,
clouds hanging far below our feet, and the vast cas-
cades tumbling down the rocks with a confused roaring,
would have been *solemnly entertaining* to me, if I had
suffered less from the extreme cold that reigns here."
If that is not Salvator Rosa in little, what is? I know
few things better, unless it be Ovid's *Nile jocose*, game-
some Nile.

No. Lady Mary's nature, like that of most of her
contemporaries, was an artful invention of trim lawns,
boxed walks, shady alleys with a statue at the end or
a ruined temple on a turfy hill. Such gardens she liked
well enough to stroll in; but the garden that charmed
her most was the garden of her soul. "Whoever will
cultivate their own mind, will find full employment.
Every virtue does not only require great care in the

planting, but as much daily solicitude in cherishing, as exotic fruits and flowers. . . . Add to this the search after knowledge (every branch of which is entertaining), and the longest life is too short for the pursuit of it."

In that pursuit she never tired, from her early youth to her latest years. Indeed, among her contemporaries she had the reputation of a learning as masculine as some of her other tastes and habits. Here rumor probably exaggerated, as usual. She herself, in her many curious and interesting references to her education, disclaims anything of the sort. She was a bright, quick child, left to herself, with a passion for reading and many books accessible. She learned Latin, French, and Italian, and used them, but rather as a reader than as a scholar. Systematic intellectual training she could hardly have had or desired, merely that passionate delight in the things of the mind which is one of the greatest blessings that can be bestowed upon a human being. "If," she says of her granddaughter, "she has the same inclination (I should say passion) for learning that I was born with, history, geography, and philosophy will furnish her materials to pass away cheerfully a longer life than is allotted to mortals."

She had, however, little disposition to brag of her acquirements. On the contrary, it is singular with what insistence, bitterness almost, she urges that a woman should never, never allow herself to be thought wiser or more studious than her kind. Read, if you please; think, if you please; but keep it to yourself. Otherwise women will laugh at you and men avoid you. "I never studied anything in my life, and have always (at least from fifteen) thought the reputation of learning a misfortune to a woman." And again, of her grand-daughter, with a sharp tang that hints at many sad experiences, "The second caution to be given her is to conceal whatever learning she attains, with as much solicitude as she would hide crookedness or lameness; the parade of it can only serve to draw on her the envy, and consequently the most inveterate hatred, of all he and she fools, which will certainly be at least three parts in four of all her acquaintance."

It is in this spirit that Lady Mary speaks very slight-ingly of her own poems and other writings; and indeed, they do not deserve much better. For us they are chiefly significant as emphasizing, in their coarseness and in some other peculiarities, that masculine strain which has been so apparent in many sides of her interesting personality.

As a critic she is more fruitful than as an author, and her remarks on contemporary writers have a singular vigor and independence. Johnson she recommends for the idle and ignorant. "Such gentle readers may be improved by a moral hint, which, though repeated over and over from generation to generation, they never heard in their lives." Fielding and Smollett she adores — again the man's taste, you see. On Clarissa she is charming. The man in her disapproves, derides. The woman weeps, "like any milkmaid of sixteen over the ballad of the Lady's Fall." But weeping, or laugh-ing, or yawning, she reads, reads, reads. For she is a true lover of books. And she thus delightfully amplifies

Montesquieu's delightful eulogy, "*Je n'ai jamais eu de chagrin qu'une demi-heure de lecture ne pouvait dissiper.*" "I wish your daughters to resemble me in nothing but the love of reading, knowing, by experience, how far it is capable of softening the cruellest accidents of life; even the happiest cannot be passed over without many uneasy hours; and there is no remedy so easy as books, which, if they do not give cheerfulness, at least restore quiet to the most troubled mind. Those that fly to cards or company for relief, generally find they only exchange one misfortune for another."

It must be by this time manifest that in the things of the spirit Lady Mary was as masculine and as stoical as in things of the flesh. In very early youth she translated Epictetus and he stood by her to the grave. Life has its vexations and many of them. People fret and torment, till even her equanimity sometimes gives way. "I am sick with vexation." But, in general, she surmounts or forgets, now with an unpleasant, haughty fling of cynical scorn, "For my part, as it is my established opinion that this globe of ours is no better than a Holland cheese, and the walkers about in it mites, I possess my mind in patience, let what will happen; and should feel tolerably easy, though a great rat came and ate half of it up;" now, as in her very last years, with a gentler reminiscence of her heroic teacher: "In this world much must be suffered, and we ought all to follow the rule of Epictetus, 'Bear and forbear.'"

As for nerves, vapors, melancholy, she has little experience of such feminine weakness, and no patience with it. "Mutability of sublunary things is the only melancholy reflection I have to make on my own account." She seldom makes any other. "Strictly speaking, there is but one real evil — I mean acute pain; all other complaints are so considerably diminished by time, that it is plain the grief of it is owing to our passion, since the sensation of it vanishes when that is over." If by chance any little wrinkle shows itself, sigh from some unknown despair, winter shadow of old age and failing strength and falling friends, let us smother it, strangle it, obliterate it, by a book, or a flower, or a smile. In these matters habit is everything.

And what was God in Lady Mary's life? Apparently, little or nothing. As strangely little as in so many eighteenth century lives. There is no rebellion, no passionate debate of hope or doubt; simply, as it seems, very little thought given to the subject. Religion is a useful thing — for the million, oh, an excellent thing, under any garb, in Turkey, in Italy, in England. Respect it? Yes. Cherish it? Yes. Believe it? The question is — well, an impertinent one. And if it be said that there may have been a feeling that some things were too sacred to be spoken about, let anyone who can read Lady Mary's letters through and retain that idea, cling to it for his comfort.

No, she lived like a gentlewoman, I had almost said like a gentleman, with a decent regard for the proprieties, a fundamental instinct of duty, a fair share of human charity, and an inexhaustible delight in the fleeting shows of time. And she died as she had lived. "Lady Mary Wortley, too, is departing," says Horace Walpole. "She brought over a cancer in her breast, which she concealed till about six weeks ago. It burst and there are no hopes of her. She behaves with great fortitude, and says she has lived long enough."

Altogether, not a winning figure, but a solid one, who, with many oddities, treads earth firmly, and makes life seem respectable, if not bewitching.

II
LADY HOLLAND

CHRONOLOGY

Elizabeth Vassall
Born March 25, 1771.
Married Sir Godfrey Webster 1786.
Traveled abroad 1791–1796.
Divorced July 4, 1797.
Married Lord Holland July 6, 1797.
Lord Holland died 1840.
Died 1845.

Elizabeth, Lady Holland

II

LADY HOLLAND

THE brilliant salons which have made so conspicuous a figure in French social life have had few counterparts in England. English women have perhaps influenced politics and thought quite as powerfully as have their French sisters. But in England the work has been done through husbands or fathers or brothers, domestically, not in an open social circle where wit glitters and ideas clash.

One of the most notable exceptions to this rule was the Holland House society during the first half of the nineteenth century. Politically Holland House was a Whig centre; but its hospitable doors were open to all who talked or thought. Fox, Canning, Brougham, Grey, Melbourne, John Russell, unbent there and discussed great themes and little. Rogers mocked, Sydney Smith laughed, Moore sang, Macaulay unwound his memory, and Greville listened and recorded. Wordsworth dropped a thought there, Talleyrand a witticism. Irving brought over the America of the eighteenth century, Ticknor of the nineteenth.

"It is the house of all Europe," says Greville. "All like it more or less; and whenever . . . it shall come to an end, a vacuum will be made in society which nothing can supply. The world will suffer by the loss; and it may be said with truth that it will 'eclipse the gaiety of nations.'" Macaulay adorned the theme with his ample rhetoric: "Former guests will recollect how many men who have guided the politics of Europe, who have moved great assemblies by reason and eloquence, who have put life into bronze or canvas, or who have left to posterity things so written that it shall not willingly let them die, were there mixed with all that was loveliest and gayest in the society of the most splendid of capitals. They will remember the peculiar character which belonged to that circle, in which every talent and accomplishment, every art and science, had its place. . . . They will remember, above all, the grace, and the kindness, far more admirable than grace, with which the princely hospitality of that ancient mansion was dispensed. They will remember the venerable and benignant countenance and the cordial voice of him who bade them welcome. . . . They will remember, too, that he whose name they hold in reverence was not less distinguished by the inflexible uprightness of his political conduct than by his loving disposition and his winning manners. They will remember that, in the last lines which he traced, he expressed his joy that he had done nothing unworthy of the friend of Fox and Grey; and they will have reason to feel similar joy, if, in looking back on many troubled years, they cannot accuse themselves of having done anything unworthy of men who were distinguished by the friendship of Lord Holland."

You will observe that little is said here of the mistress of the house. As regards Lord Holland, it is instructive to turn from Macaulay's swelling periods to

the cool comment of Greville, who was neither a
rhetorician nor a cynic: "I doubt, from all I see,
whether anybody (except his own family, including
Allen) had really a very warm affection for Lord Holland, and the reason probably is that he had none for
anybody."

There was a mistress of the house and Macaulay
elsewhere has enough to say about her. It is quite
astonishing, the unanimity with which her guests com-
bine to slight her character and emphasize her defects.
Macaulay asserts, in the passage quoted above, that
"all that was loveliest and gayest" met at Holland
House. This is quite false; for few women went there.
Those who did had little good to say of their hostess.
In the early years before she married Lord Holland,
Miss Holroyd wrote of her: "If anybody ever offends
you so grievously that you do not recollect any punishment bad enough for them, only wish them on a
party of pleasure with Lady Webster! . . . Everything
that was proposed she decidedly determined on a contrary scheme, and as regularly altered her mind in a
few hours." Long after, Fanny Kemble expresses herself quite as bitterly: "The impression she made upon
me was so disagreeable that for a time it involved every
member of that dinner party in a halo of undistin-
guishable dislike in my mind."

When the women condemn, one expects the men to
praise. In this case they do not. All alike, in milder
or harsher terms, record her acts that crushed, her
speeches that stung. The gentle Moore takes Irving to
visit her. "Lady H. said, 'What an uncouth hour to

come at,' which alarmed me a little, but she was very civil to him." Rogers told Dyce that "when she wanted to get rid of a fop, she would beg his pardon and ask him to sit little further off, adding 'there is something on your handkerchief I do not quite like.'" She observed to Rogers himself: "Your poetry is bad enough, so pray be sparing of your prose." And to Lord Porchester: "I am sorry to hear you are going to publish a poem. Can't you suppress it?"

Also they paid her back in kind, with a vim which, in gentlemen, as they all were, seems to imply immense provocation. "My lady . . . asked me how I could write those vulgar verses the other day about Hunt," writes Moore. "Asked her in turn, why she should take it for granted, if they were so vulgar, that it was I who wrote them." Croker records: "Lady Holland was saying yesterday to her assembled coterie, 'Why should not Lord Holland be Secretary for Foreign Affairs — why not as well as Lord Landsdowne for the Home Department?' Little Lord John Russell is said to have replied, in his quiet way, 'Why, they say, Ma'am, that you open all Lord Holland's letters, and the Foreign Ministers might not like *that*.'" Rogers was talking of beautiful hair. "Why, Rogers, only a few years ago I had such a head of hair that I could hide myself in it, and I've lost it all." Rogers merely answered, "What a pity!" "But with such a look and tone," says Fanny Kemble, "that an exultant giggle ran round the table at her expense." And the table was her own! To Ticknor she said "That she believed New England was originally colonized by convicts sent over from the mother country. Mr. Ticknor replied that he was not aware of it, but said he knew that some of the Vassall family — ancestors of Lady Holland — had settled early in Massachusetts." Finally, there is the almost incredible incident so vividly narrated by Macaulay. "Lady Holland is in a most extraordinary state. She came to Rogers's, with Allen, in so bad a humour that we were all forced to rally and make common cause against her. There was not a person at table to whom she was not rude; and none of us were inclined to submit. Rogers sneered; Sydney made merciless sport of her; Tom Moore looked excessively impertinent; Bobus put her down with simple, straightforward rudeness; and I treated her with what I meant to be the coldest civility. Allen flew into a rage with us all, and especially with Sydney, whose guffaws, as the Scotch say, were indeed tremendous."

One and all, they felt that the lady wished to domineer, to rule over everything and everybody, and they did not like it. "Now, Macaulay," she would say, "we have had enough of this. Give us something else." At a crowded table, when a late guest came: "Luttrell, make room." "It must be made," murmured Luttrell; "for it does not exist." "The centurion did not keep his soldiers in better order than she kept her guests," Macaulay writes. "It is to one, 'Go,' and he goeth; and to another, 'Do this,' and it is done." Some one asked Lord Dudley why he did not go to Holland House. He said that he did not choose to be tyrannized over while he was eating his dinner.

Her friends thought she wished to regulate their

29

lives, especially to regulate them in the way that suited her comfort and convenience. What could be more remarkable than the scene Macaulay describes, when she implored, ordered him to refuse his high appointment in India? "I had a most extraordinary scene with Lady Holland. If she had been as young and as handsome as she was thirty years ago, she would have turned my head. She was quite hysterical about my going; paid me such compliments as I cannot repeat; cried; raved; called me dear dear Macaulay. 'You are sacrificed to your family. I see it all. You are too good to them. They are always making a tool of you; last session about the slaves; and now sending you to India.' I always do my best to keep my temper with Lady Holland for three reasons: because she is a woman; because she is very unhappy in her health, and in the circumstances of her position; and because she has a real kindness for me. But at last she said something about you. This was too much, and I was beginning to answer her in a voice trembling with anger, when she broke out again: 'I beg your pardon. Pray forgive me, dear Macaulay. I was very impertinent. I know you will forgive me. Nobody has such a temper as you. I said so to Allen only this morning. I am sure you will bear with my weakness. I shall never see you again'; and she cried, and I cooled; for it would have been to very little purpose to be angry with her. I hear that it is not to me alone that she runs on in this way. She storms at the ministry for letting me go."

And she was supposed to tyrannize over her household as well as over her guests. The Allen referred to above is a curious figure. Originally recommended to Lord Holland as a traveling physician, he entered the family and remained in it. He was an immense reader, a careful student, and supplied many a Holland House politician with the stuff of oratory. He had opinions of his own, was a violent enemy of all religion, and was gibingly known as "Lady Holland's atheist." He did not hesitate to contradict his patroness and some even assert that she was a little afraid of him. At any rate, he was deeply attached to her, remained with her after Lord Holland's death, and suffered himself in practical matters to be ordered about like a domestic poodle. Moore records an interesting bit of mutual self-confession, when Allen, after years of intimate contact with the deepest thought and brightest wit in Europe, admitted that to keep up conversation during these evenings was "frequently a most heavy task and that if he had followed his own taste and wishes he would long since have given up that mode of life." And Moore himself adds that the "Holland House sort of existence, though by far the best specimen of its kind going, would appear to me, for any continuance, the most wearisome of all forms of slavery."

Even Lord Holland himself appeared to his observant visitors to be subject to a domination at times somewhat irksome. "A little after twelve my lady retired and intimated that he ought to do so too," writes Moore; "but he begged hard for ten minutes more." Greville says that when some revivalists called on Lord Holland, Lady Holland was with great difficulty persuaded to allow him to go and receive them.

"At last she let him be wheeled in, but ordered Edgar and Harold, the two pages, to post themselves outside the door and rush in if they heard Lord Holland scream." On the great occasion of Macaulay's going to India, it is recorded that the good-natured husband was goaded into a disciplinary outburst: "Don't talk such nonsense, my lady! What the devil! Can we tell a gentleman who has a claim upon us that he must lose his only chance for getting an independence in order that he may come and talk to you in an evening?"

I repeat, it is a most curious thing to observe this mob of illustrious and kindly gentlemen handing down to posterity such unanimous abuse of a lady, who, whatever her defects, had done them infinite courtesies. And she is dead and cannot defend herself.

She left a journal, however, which Lord Ilchester has lately edited. And few studies can be more delightful than to turn from the picture painted of her by her friends(?) to her intimate and faithful likeness of herself. The tart, even the boisterous, tongue is indeed not concealed, as when she told a political friend that "I regretted he had not lived in the Middle Ages and given his faith to orthodox points, as he would have made one of the firmest pillars of the church, instead of being a milk and water politician now." But there are many other things besides tartness and boisterousness.

Unfortunately the Journal stops before the great days of Holland House began. What would we not give for the lady's account of those conversations with Moore and Ticknor and Macaulay? What for portraits of them and of others such as she well knew how to draw? For her pen was no mean one. It could bite and sting, could emphasize lights and shadows quite as strongly as some of those that etched the figures at her table and the scenes in her drawing-room. You may meet such a type as the following any day in Italy; but only an artist could so render it. "The old Marchesa was also delightful, not to the eye, for she was hideous, nor to the ear, for she squalled, nor to the nose, for she was an Italian; yet, from her unbounded desire of pleasing, the *tout ensemble* created more agreeable sensations than many more accomplished could have inspired." Or match this with an English married couple: "The first thing she did was to live apart from him, and keep up a love correspondence with him; hence to the world they appeared enamoured of one another. She is a little mad, and parsimony is her chief turn. She is good-natured and a little clever. Trevor has no judgment and slender talents. His foibles are very harmless and his whole life has been insipidly good. His *ridicules* are a love of dress coats, *volantes*, and always speaking French. *Au reste*, he is very like other people, only better." And, as will appear from these two, her portraits, though satirical, are not all unkindly, or at least she sweetens the bitterest of them with a touch of human charity.

Just a few sketches she has of the great men who afterwards became so widely identified with her, enough to increase our ardent desire for more. Thus the following of Wordsworth, interesting in every word for both painter and painted, if somewhat astounding: "Sent an invitation to Wordsworth, one of the Lake poets, to come and dine, or visit us in the evening. He came. He is much superior to his writings, and his conversation is even beyond his abilities. I should almost fear he is disposed to apply his talents more towards making himself a *vigorous conversaticnist* in the style of our friend Sharp, than to improve his style of composition. . . . He holds some opinions on picturesque subjects with which I completely differ, especially as to the effects produced by white houses on the sides of the hills; to my taste they produce a cheerful effect. He, on the contrary, would brown, or even black-work them; he maintained his opinion with a considerable degree of ingenuity." With which compare the snub administered by Henry Taylor, when she sneered at Wordsworth's poetry: "Let me beg you to believe, Lady Holland, that this has not been the sort of thing to say about Wordsworth's poetry for the last ten years."

But the Journal is far less interesting for its portraits of others than for that of the lady herself, who is seen there complete, and human, and not unlovely.

When she was young, she was beautiful. "I observed a portrait of Lady Holland, painted some thirty years ago," says Macaulay. "I could have cried to see the change. She must have been a most beautiful woman."

A mere child, she was married to a man she detested, who perhaps deserved it. "At fifteen, through caprice and folly, I was thrown into the power of one who was a pompous coxcomb, with youth, beauty, and a good disposition, all to be so squandered!" I imagine that Sir Godfrey Webster was a rough English squire of the

Western type, fond of beef, beer, hunting, and rural politics, fond also of his wife, after his fashion, but believing that wives should bake, brew, and breed, and utterly intolerant of my lady's freaks and fancies, of her social ambitions and her sentimental whims. To her he appeared a simple brute. When he "in a paroxysm threw the book I was reading at my head, after having first torn it out of my hands," I can divine something of how he felt. So perhaps could she; but the incident gave her all the gratification of martyrdom.

"Ah; me!" she writes, "what can please or cheer one who has no hope of happiness in life? Solitude and amusement from external objects is all I hope for; home is the abyss of misery!" Condemned to the exile of a country house, I am sorry to say that she revenged herself by devising cruel tricks against her husband's aunt, who, however, was most apt at paying back. Later her despair drove her nearly to suicide. "Oftentimes in the gloom of midnight I feel a desire to curtail my grief, and but for an unaccountable shudder that creeps over me, ere this the deed of rashness would be executed. I shall leave nothing behind that I can regret. My children are yet too young to attach me to existence, and Heaven knows I have no close, no tender ties besides. Oh, pardon the audacity of the thought."

Then Lord Holland appeared and her whole life was altered. With such an early career and with a temper so erratic one would hardly expect that an irregular connection, even though legalized as soon as possible by divorce and marriage, would turn out well. It did. When she first meets her lover, he is "quite delightful." A number of years later she recognizes that life with him has transformed her character. Every hour she continues "to wonder [*sic*] and admire the most wonderful union of benevolence, sense, and integrity in the character of the excellent being whose faith is pledged with mine. Either he has imparted some of his goodness to me, or the example of his excellence has drawn out the latent good I had — as certainly I am a better person and a more useful member of society than I was in my years of misery."

Although she was still young and very beautiful, the ardent suit of other lovers makes no impression on her. She gets rid of them as best she can and consults her husband as to the most effective manner of doing so.

Formerly life was hateful and she longed to be rid of it. "In the bitterness of sorrow I prayed for death. Now I am a coward indeed; a spasm terrifies me, and every memento of the fragile tenure of my bliss strikes a panic through my frame. Oh! my beloved friend, how hast thou by becoming mine endeared the every day occurrences of life! I shrink from nothing but the dread of leaving or of losing thee." In the lot of an acquaintance who has lost her husband she bewails the most terrible of future possibilities for herself. "How fortunate for her should she never awaken to her wretchedness, but die in the agonies of delirium. Oh! in mercy let such be my close if I am doomed to the — oh! I cannot with calmness suppose the case."

It is in no cynical spirit, nor with any question of the genuineness of these feelings, but simply as a comment on the ways of this world, that I turn to a passage of

LADY HOLLAND

Greville, written three months after Lord Holland's death: "I dined with Lady Holland yesterday. Everything there is exactly the same as it used to be, excepting only the person of Lord Holland, who seems to be pretty well forgotten. The same talk went merrily round, the laugh rang loudly and frequently, and, but for the black and the mob-cap of the lady, one might have fancied he had never lived or had died half a century ago."

There has been some question as to whether Lady Holland cared very much for her children by either marriage. Certainly at her death she left her son only two thousand pounds and a large income to a comparative stranger. Yet at the time of her separation from her first husband she sought passionately to retain her daughter, even resorting to the strange and characteristic device of pretending that the child was dead and burying a kid in a coffin in her place.

The Journal, too, is full of passages that come straight from the heart and absolutely prove a sincere, if somewhat erratic maternal affection. I hardly know a stranger mixture of passionate grief and curious self-analysis than the following passage, written on occasion of a child's death. "There is a sensation in a mother's breast at the loss of an infant that partakes of the feeling of instinct. It is a species of savage despair. Alas! to lose my pretty infant, just beginning to prattle his little innocent wishes, and imagination so busily aids my grief by tracing what he might have been. In those dreary nights whilst I sat watching his disturbed sleep, I knelt down and poured out to God a fervent prayer for his recovery, and swore that if he were spared me the remainder of my life should be devoted to the exercise of religious duties; that I would believe in the mercy of a God who could listen to and alleviate my woe. Had he lived I should have been a pious enthusiast. I have no superstition in my nature, but from what I then felt it is obvious how the mind may be worked upon when weakened and perplexed by contending passions of fear, hope, and terror."

It is admitted that Lady Holland was an able housekeeper, and Mr. Ellis Roberts even thinks that the success of her salon was largely owing to the excellence of her table. "It is true the parties were overcrowded, but . . . men do not much care how they eat, if what they eat is to their liking." It is admitted, also, that she was most generous, kind, and thoughtful for her servants. Yet the inveterate prejudice against her manifests itself even here. "In this," says Greville, "probably selfish considerations principally moved her; it was essential to her comfort to be diligently and zealously served, and she secured by her conduct to them their devoted attachment. It used often to be said in joke that they were very much better off than her guests." Nevertheless, perhaps there are worse tests of character than the devoted attachment of servants.

On Lady Holland's intellectual and spiritual life much curious light is thrown by her Journal, when taken in connection with the comments of her friends. Her wayward childhood, her early marriage, her utter lack of systematic education must not be forgotten. "I should be *bien autre chose* if I had been regularly taught.

I never had any method in my pursuits, and I was always too greedy to follow a thing with any *suite*. Till lately [age 26] I did not know the common principles of grammar, and still a boy of ten years old would outdo me." Yet she was a wide, curious, and intelligent reader, and remembered what she read, as when she located one of Moore's innumerable stories in an old volume of Fabliaux.

She had her strong opinion on most general subjects. In art she was distinctly of the eighteenth century, as in her view of Wordsworth's poetry, and her admiration for Guido and the Bolognese painters. "'St. Peter weeping,' by *Guido*, reckoned the first of his works and the most faultless picture in Italy." Nature sometimes moved her deeply, however, as became a contemporary of Byron and Chateaubriand: "The weather was delicious, truly Italian, the night serene, with just enough air to waft the fragrance of the orange-flower, then in blossom. Through the leaves of the trees we caught glimpses of the trembling moonbeams on the glassy surface of the bay; all objects conspired to soothe my mind and the sensations I felt were those of ecstatic rapture. I was so happy that when I reached my bedroom, I dismissed my maid, and sat up the whole night looking from my window upon the sea."

In religion she was more than liberal, in fact, had no positive beliefs. "Oh, God! chance, nature, or whatever thou art," is the best she can do in the way of a prayer, though she never encouraged sceptical talk at her table and sometimes snubbed Allen sharply for it. With irreligion went a strong touch of superstition, as so often. "She would not set out on a journey of a Friday for any consideration; dreadfully afraid of thunder, etc.," "was frightened out of her wits by hearing a dog howl. She was sure that this portended her death, or my lord's."

According to her critical guests she was pitifully afraid of death always. "She was in a terrible taking about the cholera," writes Macaulay; "talked of nothing else; refused to eat any ice, because somebody said that ice was bad for the cholera." And again, in regard to the same disease: "Lady Holland apparently considers the case so serious that she has taken her conscience out of Allen's keeping and put it into the hands of Charles Grant." At any rate, she was morbidly, almost ludicrously anxious about her health; and she herself records that in Spain she selfishly refused to let Allen leave her when she was very ill to attend another invalid friend who greatly needed him. Yet in view of many other passages in her Journal, I cannot think that she really lacked courage in the face of death or of anything else. With her it is never possible to tell what is serious and what is whim. Certain it is that her parting scene was dignified, if not even noble: "She evinced during her illness a very philosophical calmness and resolution, and perfect good-humor, aware that she was dying, and not afraid of death."

In her main interest, she was preëminently a social being. Greville says that she dreaded solitude above everything, that she "could not live alone for a single minute; she never was alone, and even in her moments of greatest grief it was not in solitude but in society that she sought her consolation." Her Journal is, I think, sufficient to prove that this is exaggerated. She read and loved to read, and no true lover of books hates solitude. Still she was social, loved men and women and their talk and laughter, loved the sparkle of wit, the snap of repartee, the long interchange of solid argument. Nor was she too particular in the choice of her associates. "There was no person of any position in the world, no matter how frivolous and foolish, whose acquaintance she was not eager to cultivate," says Greville again. Here, too, her Journal supplies a needed correction, or at least sets things in a fairer and more agreeable light: "A long acquaintance is with me a passport to affection. This does not operate to exclusion of new acquaintances, as I seek them with avidity." The "passport to affection" is generally recognized. She was loyal in her affections and in her admirations, though sometimes carrying them, like everything else, to the point of oddity, as in her strange worship of Napoleon.

That a person so fond of society should have shown so little tact in it is one of the curious features of her case. But some things throw an interesting light on her brusqueness, her downright rudeness. Here is one brief passage about a woman she met and liked. "If I were to see much of her she might perhaps be benefited, for as nobody can do more mischief to a woman than a woman, so perhaps might one reverse the maxim and say nobody can do more good. A little mild reproof and disapprobation of some of her doctrines might possibly rescue her from the gulf." Does not that explain a host of oddities, and pleasantly? Who of us likes to be rescued from the gulf by a little mild reproof?

And the woman was nervous, sensitive, imaginative. Society irritates such people even when it fascinates them. Of one guest she writes: "His loud voice and disgusting vanity displeased me so much that I fled for refuge speedily into my own room." Another bit of most delicate analysis shows how easily the social disillusionment of a sensitive organization might manifest itself in tactless ill-humor. "There is some perverse quality in the mind that seems to take an active pleasure in destroying the amusement it promises to itself. It never fails to baffle my expectations; so sure as I propose to my imagination an agreeable conversation with a person where past experience warrants the hope, so sure am I disappointed. I feel it perpetually, for example, with Dumont; with him I have passed very many cheerful hours. This knowledge tempts me to renew our walks, the consequence is we both yawn." So clear, so sure is it, that in all human relations the true road to happiness and enjoyment is not to seek them directly for one's self.

The sense of power, of guiding and controlling others, was doubtless a large element of Lady Holland's social instinct. "Her love and habit of domination were both unbounded," writes Greville. To achieve this, to govern the sort of men that gathered about her, she knew that she must study their pursuits. Hence she devoted herself to the details of politics almost as sedulously as did Greville himself. The minuteness of her Spanish Journals, personally of little importance, in this respect, is remarkable. Yet I know of few things more delight-fully feminine than her brief comment on ministerial changes. Her friends go out of power, and she observes, "The loss of all interest in public affairs was the natural effect of the change of Administration to me."

It is, I hope, by this time evident, that, whatever her virtues or her defects, Lady Holland was an extraordinarily interesting character. I have quoted from her guests and friends much that was bitter. But a careful search brings out also testimony all the more favorable when we consider the extent of the abuse. Thus Greville admits that "though often capricious and impertinent, she was never out of temper, and bore with good-humor and calmness the indignant and resentful outbreaks which she sometimes provoked in others." And while asserting that "She was always intensely selfish," he adds in the next sentence that "To those who were ill and suffering, to whom she could show any personal kindness and attention, among her intimate friends, she never failed to do so." Sydney Smith writes to her with a tenderness, an obviously genuine affection, which would prove fine qualities in any woman: "I am not always confident of your friendship for me at particular times; but I have great confidence in it from one end of the year to the other: above all, I am confident that I have a great affection for you." "I have heard five hundred people assert that there is no such agreeable house in Europe as Holland House: why should you be the last person to be convinced of this and the first to make it true?" "I love the Hollands so much that I would go to them in any spot, however innocent, sequestered and rural." Finally, the most sympathetic, as well as one of the shrewdest judgments, comes from Sir Henry Holland, the physician, who had studied Lady Holland in all her aspects perhaps as carefully as any one. "In my long and intimate knowledge of Lady Holland, I never knew her to desert an old friend, whatever his condition might be. Many things seemingly wilful and incongruous in her might be explained through this happier quality of mind blended with that love of power, which, fostered by various circumstances, pervaded every part of her life. . . . Her manner of conversation at the dinner-table — sometimes arbitrary and in rude arrest of others, sometimes courteously inviting the subject — furnished a study in itself. Every guest felt her presence, and generally more or less succumbed to it. She was acute in distinguishing between real and false merit, and merciless in her treatment of the latter. Not a woman of wit in words, she had what might well be called consummate wit in all her relations to society. Once only, and that very late in life, she spoke to me of the labor she underwent in maintaining the position thus acquired."

May we not accept Greville's dictum that she was a very strange woman, adding that, after all, she played her rôle of a great lady in not unseemly fashion? And perhaps it was with some justice that on her deathbed she spoke — most characteristically — of her life "with considerable satisfaction, asserting that she had done as much good and as little harm as she could during her existence."

III
MISS AUSTEN

CHRONOLOGY

Jane Austen.

Born December 16, 1775.

Wrote "Pride and Prejudice," 1796–1797.

"Sense and Sensibility," published 1811.

"Pride and Prejudice," published 1813.

"Mansfield Park," published 1814.

"Emma," published 1816.

Died July 18, 1817.

"Northanger Abbey" and "Persuasion," published 1818.

Jane Austen

III

MISS AUSTEN

JANE AUSTEN lived her brief life in two or three quiet English towns. She had no adventures, no experiences, no great fortunes or misfortunes. She began to do her best writing when she was little more than a girl. She left a few immortal works, surpassed by no others in the painting of the human heart. What sort of woman was she herself? Not very remarkable to look at, it appears. Round, full cheeks — "for the most part, they are foolish that are so," Cleopatra tells us — bright, hazel eyes, brown curls about her face. No doubt, in every point a lady. But her soul?

At first sight, it seems that she laughed, mocked, at all things, very gently and decorously, but still mocked. "I dearly love a laugh," says the heroine who surely most resembles her creatress. And again it is said of this same Elizabeth Bennett: "She had a lively, playful disposition which delighted in anything ridiculous."

Those who love Miss Austen best will recognize, far beyond any testimony of quoted instances, this incessant, pervading spirit of gentle mockery which appears in all her books, courteous, infinitely well-bred, but sometimes very far from amiable.

That she should mock at woman's education was, perhaps, at the beginning of the nineteenth century, natural enough. But it would be hard to find any one in any century who has mocked at it more cruelly. "Where people wish to attach, they should always be ignorant. To come with a well-informed mind is to come with an inability of administering to the vanity of others, which a sensible person would always wish to avoid. A woman, especially, if she have the misfortune of knowing anything, should conceal it as well as she can." Which was also the opinion of Lady Mary Wortley Montagu, considered one of the most learned women of her time. Now we have changed all that.

But if you suppose that Miss Austen wishes to contrast with learning the sweets of domesticity, you are far astray indeed. I do not know whether she read La Rochefoucauld. She hardly needed to. In any case, she well supports his dictum that there are comfortable marriages, but no delicious ones. The motive of most she lashes with her whip of silken scorn. "His temper might perhaps be a little soured by finding, like many others of his sex, that through some unaccountable bias in favor of beauty, he was the husband of a very silly woman." Though she had a sister whom she loved better than anything on earth, the kindest thing she could find to say of two most affectionate sisters was: "Among the merits and the happiness of Elinor and Marianne, let it not be ranked as the least considerable, that, though sisters, and living almost within sight of each other, they could live without disagreement between themselves, or producing coolness between their husbands."

Nor is she much more enthusiastic about the charms of society. Her heroines do, indeed, love an outing or a ball; but much more stress is laid on untoward accidents that blight enjoyment than on its rapturous completeness. And this is life, as we all know. Only — As for the little distresses of social converse, who has ever depicted them more subtly? "To Elizabeth it appeared, that had her family made an agreement to expose themselves as much as they could during the evening, it would have been impossible for them to play their parts with more spirit, or finer success."

No one probably will maintain that Miss Austen treats love very seriously. Its common youthful ardors, "what is so often described as arising on a first interview with its object, and even before two words have been exchanged," she makes matter for derision or dismisses with indifference. Isabella utters a platitude on the subject. "This charming sentiment, recommended as much by sense as novelty, gave Catherine a most pleasing remembrance of all the heroines of her acquaintance." With the author's own serious heroines love is an emotion of such reverend profundity that the ladies themselves require years to discover it, and even then it has to be forced upon their notice.

Religion and the deeper concerns of life generally, where they are mentioned at all, fare no better. They are touched with an irony of somewhat dubious effect on the profane, as at the end of Northanger Abbey, where those it may concern are left to wonder "Whether the tendency of this work be altogether to recommend parental tyranny, or reward filial disobedience." There is no doubt, however, that Miss Austen sincerely honored sacred things. She would have said with her own

Elizabeth, "I hope I never ridicule what is wise or good." She appeared to think she would attain this end by keeping matters of the soul mainly out of her work. But she miscalculated a little. I do not know how one could more discredit religion than by exhibiting it in such representatives as Dr. Grant, Mr. Elton, and Mr. Collins: a glutton, a ninny, and an imbecile. If any reader holds that the prosy sermonizing of Edward Bertram helps the divine end of the matter, I disagree totally.

And as she mocked all things in human life, so she had a peculiar fancy for mocking the departure out of it. We know much mockable is there; but it seems odd matter for a young girl to deal with. "It was felt as such things must be felt. Everybody had a degree of gravity and sorrow; tenderness toward the departed, solicitude for the surviving friends; and, in a reasonable time, curiosity to know where she would be buried. Goldsmith tells us that when lovely woman stoops to folly, she has nothing to do but to die; and when she stoops to be disagreeable, it is equally to be recommended as a clearer of ill-fame."

Obviously Miss Austen's mocking was not all sweet, sunny, natural gaiety. It had too much ill-nature in it. This shows, I think, in her fundamental conception of character. Read over her list of *dramatis personæ* and see how many are attractive or agreeable. It is not that she presents set types of evil or folly. Far from it. Her people are all human, vividly human, walking figures of flesh and blood humanity. But like all true human beings, they have good and evil both, and her vision usually turns towards the evil, the mildly evil, the foolish and ridiculous. This perversion is slight, but constant, and its very slightness makes it more true — and more depressing. What doubles the hideousness of the hideous scene between Mr. and Mrs. Dashwood ("Sense and Sensibility," chapter ii) is its perfect humanity and the possibility that it might have been you and I.

She will brand a whole company with a touch: they "almost all labored under one or other of these disqualifications for being agreeable — want of sense, either natural or improved — want of elegance — want of spirits — or want of temper." As any company might, to be sure — if you took it so. She will brand a whole sex. Mr. Palmer had "no traits at all unusual in his sex and time of life. He was nice in his eating, uncertain in his hours; fond of his child, though affecting to slight it; and idled away the morning at billiards, which ought to have been devoted to business."

Above all, she is severe upon women past middle life. Few indeed has she drawn that are even tolerable. Yet I have known some who were charming. With what infinite, subtle, loving art are Mrs. Jennings and Mrs. Norris made odious! And the best illustration of all for Miss Austen's methods is Miss Bates. Her creatress starts with a heroic determination to be amiable for once. God has given this poor old specimen excellent qualities. For heaven's sake, let us dwell upon them and leave the defects in shadow. "She was a happy woman, and a woman whom no one named without good will. It was her own universal good will and contented temper which worked such wonders. She loved everybody, was interested in everybody's happiness, quick-sighted to everybody's merits." Yet the turning of a page makes Miss Bates ridiculous, and the turning of more makes her almost as tedious to us as the author evidently found her. In the end she drives even Emma to open insult, which Emma speedily regrets, and would probably as speedily renew.

But, it will be urged, I am making the old mistake of interpreting an author from her writings, of transferring to her the sentiments of her characters, or, at any rate, her merely formal literary expression.

Very well, let us turn to Miss Austen's letters, and see what we find there. To begin with, they are charming letters, full of life, spirit, and vivacity, quite as charming as her novels. Her editors and biographers seem to feel it necessary to apologize for them. Why? It is true, they contain no reference to topics of the day. She might never have heard of Napoleon, or known that America was discovered. But, as letters, they are none the worse for that. Also, they are not formally literary, have no set pieces, or elaborate disquisitions. There is hardly a general thought in the whole of them. Who cares? They are literary as being the work of one of the most exquisite masters of expression. Indeed, an occasional odd glimpse of her constant literary preoccupation slips out. "Benjamin Portal is here. How charming that is! I do not know exactly why, but the phrase followed so naturally that I could not help putting it down." And again: "Your letter is come. It

came, indeed, twelve lines ago, but I could not stop to
acknowledge it before, and I am glad it did not arrive
till I had completed my first sentence, because the
sentence had been made ever since yesterday, and I
think forms a very good beginning." But, in general,
they are merely the swiftest, lightest chronicle of little
daily happenings, made eternal by a sense of fun as
keen as Lamb's. Is there in Lamb any bit of happier
nonsense than the sketch of Mr. Haden? "You seem
to be under a mistake as to Mr. H. You call him an
apothecary. He is no apothecary; he has never been an
apothecary; there is not an apothecary in this neigh-
bourhood. . . . He is a Haden, nothing but a Haden,
a sort of wonderful nondescript creature on two legs,
something between a man and an angel, but without
the least spice of an apothecary. He is, perhaps, the
only person *not* an apothecary hereabouts. He has
never sung to us. He will not sing without a pianoforte
accompaniment."

Yet, minute as they are, and natural as they are,
Miss Austen's letters tell us little about herself, that is,
the inmost self that we wish to get at. Those we have
were almost all written to her nearest and dearest sister, Cassandra. To Cassandra, if to any one, she must
have opened her soul. But, if so, she did it by lip and
not by letter. It is rare indeed that she goes so far as to
say, "I am sick of myself and my bad pens." To be
sure, such concealment of personal feeling and emotion
is a most significant trait of character. The gleam and
glitter of those sparkling pages with all their implica-
tion and suggestion recalls the charming speech of Birn-

heim to Fanny Lear, "*Ce qui fait le charme de votre conversation, ce n'est pas seulement ce que vous dites; c'est
encore et surtout ce que vous ne dites pas.*" But when
we try to get any definite picture of the writer, she
eludes us like a kind of elfin spirit, in perpetual glim-
mering, mazy dance, refusing to stand still.

At any rate, mockery is the prominent feature in the
letters, as in the novels; and in letters as in novels, the
mockery, though sometimes sunny and sweet, is too
often unkindly and leaves a sting. Miss Austen herself
once at least recognizes this. She describes a certain
person as "the sort of woman who gives me the idea of
being determined never to be well and who likes her
spasms and nervousness, and the consequence they
give her, better than anything else. This is an ill-
natured statement to send all over the Baltic." Doubtless, her modesty prevented her from thinking of the
ill-natured statements she was to send for ages all over
the world.

But let us see, again, with more minuteness how
completely she spins this gauze web of satire over every
phase of life. Is learning in question? "I think I may
boast myself to be, with all possible vanity, the most
unlearned and uninformed female who ever dared to be
an authoress." Or is she discussing family relations?
"The possessor of one of the finest estates in England
and of more worthless nephews and nieces than any
other private man in the United Kingdom." A pro-
spective marriage is summarily disposed of. Mr.
Blackall is "a piece of perfection — noisy perfection.
. . . I could wish Miss Lewis to be of a silent turn and

rather ignorant, but naturally intelligent and wishing to learn, fond of cold veal pies, green tea in the afternoon, and a green window-blind at night." Mrs. Austen is disturbed by receiving an unamiable letter from a relative. Miss Austen is not. "The discontentedness of it shocked and surprised her — but *I* see nothing in it out of nature."

As to society she resembles her heroines in liking balls, and, like her heroines, she finds many drawbacks in them. "Our ball was chiefly made up of Jervoises and Terrys, the former of whom were apt to be vulgar, the latter to be noisy. . . . I had a very pleasant evening, however, though you will probably find out that there was no particular reason for it; but I do not think it worth while to wait for enjoyment until there is some real opportunity for it." On beauty she comments freely. "There were very few beauties, and such as there were were not very handsome. Miss Iremonger did not look well, and Mrs. Blount was the only one much admired. She appeared exactly as she did in September, with the same broad face, diamond bandeau, white shoes, pink husband, and fat neck." As in this passage, she often refers to dress and too often unkindly. "Mrs. Powlett was at once expensively and nakedly dressed; we have had the satisfaction of estimating her lace and her muslins; and she said too little to afford us much other amusement." In regard to one special company she seems to express naïvely her general attitude. "I cannot anyhow continue to find people agreeable."

More intimate social relations and the sacred name

of friendship are treated at least as lightly. "The neighborhood have quite recovered the death of Mrs. Rider; so much so, that I think they are rather rejoiced at it now; her things were so very dear! And Mrs. Rogers is to be all that is desirable. Not even death itself can fix the friendships of the world."

And love? Persons who mock at nothing else mock at that. What should we expect, then, from the genius of mockery? Whether she rallied her young men to their faces, I do not know. Assuredly she rallied them behind their backs. One evening she expects an offer, but is determined to refuse, unless he promises to give away his white coat. The next she makes over to a friend all her love interest, even "the kiss which C. Powlett wanted to give me," everything except Tom Lefroy, "for whom I don't care sixpence." And when, writing to her niece in later years, she sketches the man she might have loved, she ends by turning all into laughter. "There are such beings in the world, perhaps one in a thousand, as the creature you and I should think perfection, where grace and spirit are united to worth, where the manners are equal to the heart and understanding, but such a person may not come in your way, or, if he does, he may not be the eldest son of a man of fortune, the near relation of your particular friend and belonging to your own county."

Also, as in the novels, she is perpetually laughing at religion and virtue, that is, of course, at those elements in religion and virtue which are undeniably laughable. Morals and immorals she can treat lightly in individual cases. "The little flaw of having a mistress now living

with him at Ashdown Park seems to be the only un-
pleasing circumstance about him." In their general
phases she can jumble them happily with physical disorders. "What is become of all the shyness in the
world? Moral as well as natural diseases disappear in
the progress of time, and new ones take their place.
Shyness and the sweating sickness have given way to
confidence and paralytic complaints." On death she
is inexhaustible. One would think she found it the
most humorous thing in life — as perhaps it is. With
what amiable, kid-gloved atrocity does she bury Mrs.
Holder. "Only think of Mrs. Holder's being dead!
Poor woman, she has done the only thing in the world
she could possibly do to make one cease to abuse her."
Apparently, even this supreme effort of Mrs. Holder's
was not successful, in fact embalmed her in spiced
abuse forever. Other interments are quite as sympathetic as hers.

Most curious of all is Miss Austen on the death of a
near relative, the trim decorum, the correct restraint,
the evident fear of being either over-conventional or
under-feeling. So in the first letter; but two days later
she rebounds and trifles with her mourning. "*One* Miss
Baker makes my gown and the other my bonnet, which
is to be silk covered with crape." Well could she say of
herself, "I can lament in one sentence and laugh in the
next." Only she immensely mistook the proportion.

One bare strong phrase takes us right to the root of
all the mocking and perversity. "Pictures of perfection, as you know, make me sick and wicked."

It is in this spirit that she makes fun even of her own

art, novel writing, will not take it seriously, "the art of keeping lovers apart in five volumes," will not take its professors seriously. She mocks at their machinery, their heroines, their landscape, their morals, and their language, "novel slang," she calls it, "thorough novel slang, and so old that I daresay Adam met with it in the first novel he opened." Whatever pains she may have taken with her own work, she does not mention them, unless ironically, when some one praises her. "I am looking about for a sentiment, an illustration, or a metaphor in every corner of the room." If money and profit are suggested as possible objects, she laughs at them. Fame is all she is thinking of. "I write only for fame and without any view to pecuniary emolument." But when it is a question of glory, she laughs at that, and toils instead for pounds and shillings. "Though I like praise as well as anybody, I like what Edward calls *Pewter*, too." Yet at the getting of money, and at the keeping of it, and at the spending of it, and at the lack of it, still she laughs: "They will not come often, I dare say. They live in a handsome style and are rich, and she seemed to like to be rich, and we gave her to understand that we were far from being so; she will soon feel, therefore, that we are not worth her acquaintance."

One subject only is too sacred for mocking — the British navy. And even that seems sacred chiefly in connection with the Austens; for Sir Walter Elliot is allowed to say that all officers should be killed off after forty because of their weatherbeaten complexion. Miss Austen herself, however, appears to have been possessed, like Louisa Musgrove, with "a fine naval fervour," which blossoms in Captain Wentworth's rapturous praise of his calling and fruits in the charming conclusion of "Persuasion": "She gloried in being a sailor's wife, but she must pay the tax of quick alarm for belonging to that profession which is, if possible, more distinguished in the domestic virtues than in its national importance." A sentiment which would have delighted Sir Joseph Porter, K.C.B., though it would have obliged Nelson to turn away his face.

So, are we to set down this demure, round-faced chit of a parson's daughter as one of the universal mockers, *der Geist der verneint* in petticoats, a sister of Aristophanes and Heine? It sounds ridiculous? How she would have shrunk from *Das Buch Le Grand* and shuddered with horror at *Schnabelwopski!* Yet would she?

But her cynicism is more nearly related to Fielding and Smollett and to the eighteenth century, that is, it does not flow from Heine's universal dissolution of all things, but is founded on a secure basis of conventional belief. Minds of that eighteenth-century type were so confident of God that they felt entirely at liberty to abuse man; "whatever is is right" said the "one infallible Pope," as Miss Austen styles him, therefore there could be no harm in calling it wrong.

On the other hand, what separates Miss Austen from Fielding, what brings her close to Heine, and what almost, if not quite, makes up for all her mocking, is that you feel underneath the mocking an infinite fund of tenderness, a warm, loving, hoping, earnest heart. Rarely has a woman been more misjudged by another woman than Miss Austen by Miss Brontë when she wrote, "Jane Austen was a complete and most sensible lady, but a very incomplete and insensible woman." Oh, no, under that demure demeanor was hidden the germ of every emotion known to woman or to man. She knew them all, she felt them all, and she restrained them all, which means quite as much character — if perhaps not quite so much "temperament" — as the volcanic flare of Charlotte Brontë. The very difficulty of tracing these things under Miss Austen's vigilant reserve adds to their significance when found and to the convincing force of their reality.

First, as to emotion in general. The testimony of the novels is often disputed. It is disputable when it refers to particular experiences and must be used with care. But many little touches would have been absolutely impossible, if the writer had not first felt them herself. Thus, she says: "It is the misfortune of poetry to be seldom safely enjoyed by those who enjoy it completely, and the strong feelings which alone can estimate it truly are the very feelings which ought to taste it but sparingly." Or again, with brief and rapid analysis, "She read with an eagerness which hardly left her the power of comprehension; and from impatience of knowing what the next sentence might bring, was incapable of attending to the sense of the one before her eyes." Do you suppose the writer of that had never torn the heart out of a letter as madly as Jane Eyre? And was there not plenty of emotion in the woman who described the moment of release from a disagreeable partner as "ecstasy," and who fainted dead away when told suddenly that she was to leave her old home and seek a new one?

Or in another line, how all the mockery of her own writing withers before one short sentence which shows the real author, like all other authors: "I *should* like to know what her estimate is, but am always half afraid of finding a clever novel *too clever*, and of finding my own story and my own people all forestalled."

Then as to love. Here the problem is more obscure. Some critics have endeavored to deduce Miss Austen's feelings from that of her heroines. Others have entirely denied the legitimacy of such deduction. No doubt, observation and divination may do much, but it seems to me that the subtle details introduced in many a critical moment must be based on experiences closely akin to those described. No man can ever understand Miss Austen's taste in heroes, and her creations in this line are the worst of her mockeries, all the more so because unintentional. But if she was blind to the faults of the type, she may have been equally blind to them in some real Edward or Knightley. We all are. I should even like to believe, with her adoring relative, that that shadowy lover who died unnamed to posterity blighted her literary effort and accounted for the singular gap between her earlier and later work. "That her grief should have silenced her is, I think, quite consistent with the reserve of her character," writes the said relative. I agree as to the possibility, but somewhat question the fact.

With the more common domestic and social feelings we are on surer ground. There is a universal concordance of testimony as to Miss Austen's sweetness in such relations, her tenderness, her charm. Guarded as her letters are, these qualities appear, in all the laughter, in all the mockery. She watches over her mother, she longs for every detail about her brothers, she cries for joy at their promotion, she exchanges with her sister a thousand little intimacies, all the more sincere for their daily triviality. It is said that the family were always amiable in their daily intercourse, never argued or spoke harshly, and I can believe it. It is said that Cassandra always controlled her temper, but that Jane had no temper to control, and the latter statement I do not believe, but do believe that appearances justified it. It is said that she loved children, and many passages in her letters prove this. See in the following the deep and evident tenderness turning into her eternal mockery. "My dear itty Dordy's remembrance of me is very pleasing to me — foolishly pleasing, because I know it will be over so soon. My attachment to him will be more durable. I shall think with tenderness and delight on his beautiful and smiling countenance and interesting manner until a few years have turned him into an ungovernable ungracious fellow."

That she enjoyed playing the rôle of maiden aunt I see no reason to imagine. But she accepted it with sweet kindliness, and as years went on, she seems to have grown even more self-forgetful and thoughtful of those about her. I have spoken of Heine. What could be lovelier than his efforts to spare his old mother every detail of his last torturing illness, writing her the gayest of letters from his pillow of agony? Everything with

MISS AUSTEN

Miss Austen is on a slighter scale; but how sweet is the story of the sofa. Sofas were scarce in those days. The Austen rooms contained but one, and Jane, dying, propped herself on two chairs, and left the sofa to her invalid mother, declaring that the chairs were preferable.

And if she loved others, they loved her. Her brother makes the truly astonishing statement that in regard to her neighbors "even on their vices did she never trust herself to comment with unkindness. . . . She always sought in the faults of others something to excuse, to forgive or forget." And he adds, "No one could be often in her company without feeling a strong desire of obtaining her friendship and cherishing a hope of having obtained it." The profound affection of her sister Cassandra needs no further evidence than the pathetic letters written by her after Jane's death, and the feeling of the other members of the family seems to have been hardly less deep. Especially was her society cherished by children and young people. "Her first charm to children was great sweetness of manner," writes her niece, "she seemed to love you, and you loved her in return." Again, "Soon came the delight of her playful talk. She could make everything amusing to a child." And later, when years had somewhat diminished the difference of age, "It had become a habit with me to put by things in my mind with reference to her, and to say to myself, I shall keep that for aunt Jane."

Altogether, whatever may have been her instincts of intellectual cynicism, she was past question a woman exquisitely lovable and one who craved and appreciated love, even when she made least show of doing so. How pathetic is the tenderness of her last letter! "As to what I owe her, and the anxious affection of all my beloved family on this occasion, I can only cry over it, and pray God to bless them more and more." And again: "If ever you are ill, may you be as tenderly nursed as I have been. May the same blessed alleviations of anxious friends be yours; and may you possess, as I dare say you will, the greatest blessing of all, in the consciousness of not being unworthy of their love. *I* could not feel this." Surely those with such a longing and with such a sense of unworthiness are not the least worthy of love in this harsh, self-absorbed, and loveless world.

Nevertheless, what remains most characteristic of Miss Austen is her singular and inexhaustible delight in the observation of humanity. No one illustrates better than she the odd paradox that it is possible to love mankind as a whole, or, at any rate, to take the greatest interest in them, while finding most individual specimens unattractive and even contemptible. I think she would have understood perfectly that wonderful passage in a letter of another novelist not unlike her, Mrs. Craigie: "I live in a world and among beings of my own creation, and when I hear of tangible mortals, what they do, what they say, and what they think, I feel a stranger and a pilgrim; life frightens me; humanity terrifies me; perhaps that is why it is real suffering for me to be in a room with more than one other. I believe I am a lover of souls, but people scare me out of my wits: it is not that I am nervous. I have only a sensation of being, as it were, in 'the wrong Paradise.' I am not at home: I talk about things I do not believe in to people who do not believe me: I become constrained, artificial."

"I am a great wonderer," says one of Miss Austen's characters. I think she was a great wonderer herself.

How fertile this interest in human nature was, what endless and richly varied entertainment it afforded, is made manifest in many passages throughout both novels and letters. "I did not know before," says Bingley to Elizabeth, "that you were a studier of character. It must be an amusing study." Elizabeth's creatress found it so. When she visits picture galleries, she confesses that she cannot look at the pictures for the men and women. In trying social situations the watchful critical instinct remains imperturbable and revels in the unguarded display of emotions commonly concealed. "Anything like a breach of punctuality was a great offense, and Mr. Moore was very angry, which I was rather glad of. I wanted to see him angry." Even in the most solemn crises the habit of curious observation cannot be wholly extinguished. Writing to her sister, with deep and genuine sympathy, on occasion of a sister-in-law's death, she interjects this query, which strikes you like a flat slap on an unexpectant cheek. "I suppose you see the corpse? How does it appear?" Finally, like all profound, minute observers of character, she realizes how far from perfect her knowledge is, that she cannot predict, cannot foresee. "Nobody ever feels or acts, suffers or enjoys, as one expects."

PORTRAITS OF WOMEN

Miss Austen alone would be sufficient to disprove the contention that age and wide knowledge of the world are necessary for the understanding of the human heart. She had neither of these qualifications. Yet, though she may have missed many superficial varieties of experience, who knew better the essential motives that animate us all? She lived in a quiet neighborhood and saw comparatively few specimens; but those were enough. As she says, through Elizabeth, "people alter so much, that there is something new to be observed in them forever."

Thus she herself enjoyed and pointed out to others the simplest, the most available, the most inexhaustible of all earthly distractions. Only, I could wish she might have seen mankind a little more constantly by the amiable side. As Lamb well observed, the great majority of Shakespeare's characters are lovable. How few of Miss Austen's are! Yet it may be that at twenty-one she knew better than Shakespeare.

IV
Madame D'Arblay

CHRONOLOGY

Frances Burney.
Born June 13, 1752.
"Evelina," published January, 1778.
"Cecilia," published July, 1782.
At Court 1786–1791.
Married General D'Arblay July 31, 1793.
"Camilla," published 1796.
"The Wanderer," published 1814.
Died January 6, 1840.

Madame D'Arblay

IV

MADAME D'ARBLAY

FRANCES BURNEY (MADAME D'ARBLAY) wrote a diary or diary-like letters almost from the cradle to the grave. For reasons which will appear later we do not know so much about her intimate self as might be expected from such minuteness of record; but her external life, the places she dwelt in, the people she saw, the things she did, are brought before us with a full detail which is rare in the biography of women and even of men.

She was by no means a Bohemian in soul. Yet her career has something of the nomadic, kaleidoscopic character which we are apt to call Bohemian. She met all sorts of people and portrayed all sorts, from the top of society to the bottom. And through this infinite diversity of spiritual contact she carried an eager eye, an untiring pen, and a singularly amiable heart.

Her father, Dr. Charles Burney, the musician and historian of music, had an excellent stock of what is nowadays called temperament. He was witty, gay, and charming. Everybody went to his house and he to everybody's. Thus Fanny in her youth (she was born in 1752) had the opportunity of seeing many of the distinguished men and women of eighteenth-century London: Johnson and Goldsmith, Sir Joshua Reynolds, Händel, Garrick and Sheridan, Bruce the traveler, actors, singers, beaux, divines, ladies with blue stockings, and with stockings of other colors. It was a gay and variegated world for a quick-eyed girl to make merry in. She made merry in it, she studied it, and as a certain literary gift was born in her, she profited.

Then, when she was twenty-five, she wrote and published anonymously an epistolary novel called "Evelina." Even to-day, though its charm is of a peculiarly perishable order, the book may be read with pleasure and some laughter. But its freshness, its ease, and its rollicking spirits must have commended it highly to an age whose own speech and manners were reflected in it. Fanny had first the delicious satisfaction of hearing genuine praise from those who had no idea of her authorship. And when the authorship was confessed — as who, under such circumstances would have concealed it? — the praise became universal, more high-pitched still, and perhaps no less delicious. The book was read everywhere, commended everywhere. Fanny's father, whom she adored, was bewitched with it. No less so was that odd personage Samuel Crisp, almost equally adored, who, like some others, having made a notable failure in literature himself, felt especially qualified to advise those who had succeeded.

In the houses where Fanny had before been a minor personage, a petted child, watching great doings and bewigged celebrities with wide-eyed curiosity from quiet corners, she now appeared as a celebrity herself, not bewigged, but with the wigs bowing down to her. Titles of honor begged for an introduction and titles of learning. She was pointed out in the streets and in the theatres. Her characters were cited, her wit quoted, her sentiments applied by daily personages to daily life. London was all the English world then and a book read by ten thousand people in London had a sort of personal success which no book could have anywhere to-day.

Best of all, Fanny was praised to her face by those whose praise she knew to be really worth having. Sir Joshua said he would give fifty pounds to know the author of "Evelina." Burke sat up all night to finish it. Murphy and Sheridan entreated her to write a comedy and Sheridan agreed to take it before a word was put on paper. To a girl of twenty-five, up to that day merely one of the babes and sucklings, all this must have seemed like a golden dream.

But the best was Johnson. Fanny was brought into intimate contact with him in Mrs. Thrale's hospitable house at Streatham. Something of the Doctor's enthusiasm must doubtless be laid to the influence of grace, beauty, and feminine charm on that ogrish and susceptible heart. But, whatever the cause, he set no bounds to an outcry of admiration sufficient to turn the head of an older and sedater woman. Nothing like "Evelina," he said, had appeared for years. And of its author "I know none like her — nor do I believe there is, or ever was, a man who could write such a book so young." And the literary praise was mingled with expressions of personal affection. "Afterwards, grasping my hand with the most affectionate warmth, he said: 'I wish you success! my dear little Burney!' When, at length, I told him I could stay no longer, and bid him good night, he said, 'There is none like you, my dear little Burney! there is none like you! — good night, my darling!'"

In such a highly-flavored atmosphere did the girl live until the publication of her second novel, "Cecilia," in 1782. This, though more elaborate, more Johnsonian, and less freshly entertaining than "Evelina," was equally well received, and Miss Burney continued to be idolized by all the literary set of London.

Then there came an extraordinary change. Mrs. Thrale married the Italian musician, Piozzi, and the Streatham circle was broken up. Miss Burney's greatest supporter, Johnson, died in 1784, and in the following year Fanny was transplanted, elevated or degraded, as you please, from the free, fascinating life of a popular author to be a personal attendant on the queen. Dr. Burney thought his daughter's future assured in the most promising fashion. She herself entered upon her new career with anxiety and regret and found nothing in it to contradict her unpleasant expectations.

The queen and princesses were, indeed, kind to her; but their hangers-on were not, or not all of them. She had been born free, had grown up in freedom, had been accustomed to indulge her fancies, to have them indulged by others, limiting them only by love and the affectionate wish to comply with the fancies of those dear to her. Now she was cramped in every movement, what was far worse, in every thought. To do servant's work for a servant's stipend was hateful. To run at bell-call for an idle bidding was more hateful. But these were nothing compared to having no home, no time, no life, of one's own. To move by the clock, some one else's clock, to be thrown into any quarters that could be spared from the needs of those higher, to dress and undress at stated times in stated fashions, to be never, never Dr. Burney's daughter, but always the handmaid of the queen — what a change from the caresses of Johnson and the compliments of Burke! Even pastimes not unwelcome in themselves become so in such surroundings. What a wail does she utter over the daily infliction of piquet with the tyrannous Mrs. Schwellenberg: "And — O picquet — life hardly hangs on earth during its compulsion, in these months succeeding months, and years creeping, crawling after years."

And then another change, quite as violent as the preceding. Miss Burney's health fails under the strain, she leaves the court, is thrown among a group of French *émigrés*, meets General D'Arblay, marries him, and settles down in a quiet country cottage, with a bit of an income and a garden full of cabbages. No Burkes or Johnsons here, no kings or queens or saucy gentlemen in waiting; just quiet. One would think she would miss it all, even what was hateful. Charles Lamb sighed to be rid of his India House slavery, and when he was rid of it, could not tell what to do with his freedom. So it is apt to be with all of us. But Madame D'Arblay apparently knew when she was well off. She adored her husband. She was absorbed in her son. She wrote another novel, "Camilla," less readable than the others, but well paid for. She entertained with perfect simplicity any friend who could come to her. She had but one dread — lest some call of military or political duty in France might draw away her husband and break up her Paradise. "Ah, if peace would come without, what could equal my peace within!"

The call of duty did come. Her husband went and she followed him, into other scenes, still totally different from what had gone before. She saw the France of the first Napoleon and Napoleon himself. She saw the restoration of the Bourbons. She was hurried along in the mad bustle of the flight from Paris. She waited in Brussels through the suspense of Waterloo. With husband and son, and alone, she had adventures and perils by land and sea. Surely she had need of a good stock of peace within, for peace without seemed very far away.

But the last act passed quietly at home in England. She was not fêted or flattered any more, as she had been. Yet enough of old glory clung about her to bring her a large price for one more very indifferent novel, "The Wanderer." Her husband died, her son died. Not much was left to her but memories and these, when she was nearly eighty, she wove into a life of her father, which Macaulay condemned, but which has at least the merit of being sweet and sunshiny. To recall such a golden past, such a tangled web of fortune, at eighty, without a word of bitterness for the present, shows a heart worth loving, worth studying. Let us study Madame D'Arblay's.

‾She will not help us so much as we could wish. "Poor Fanny's face tells what she thinks, whether she will or no," said Dr. Burney. Her face might. Her Diary does not. To be sure, she herself asserts repeatedly that she writes nothing but the truth. "How truly does this Journal contain my real, undisguised thoughts . . . its truth and simplicity are its sole recommendation." No doubt she believed so. No doubt she aimed to be absolutely veracious. No doubt she avoids false statements and perversion of fact. Her diary may be true, but it is not genuine. It is literary, artificial, in every line of it. She sees herself exactly as a man — or woman — sees himself in a mirror: the very nature of the observation involves unconscious and instinctive posing.

Macaulay, in his rhetorical fashion, draws a violent contrast between Madame D'Arblay's Memoirs of her father and her Diary. The Diary, he says, is fresh and natural, the Memoirs tricked up with all the artifice of a perfumer's shop. Neither is fresh and natural. The Memoirs are overloaded with Johnsonian ornament; but the simpler style of the Diary is not one bit more spontaneous or more genuine. It was impossible for the woman to look at herself from any but a literary point of view.

Take, for instance, the address to "Nobody," with which the Diary opens. It sets the note at once. There is not the slightest suggestion of a sincere, direct effort to record the experiences of a soul; merely an airy, literary coquetting with somebody, everybody, under the Nobody mask.

A single breath of fresh air is enough to blast the artificiality of the whole thing. Turn from a page of the Diary to any letter of Mrs. Piozzi — some of them are given in the Diary itself. A coarse woman, a passionate woman, a jealous woman — but, oh, so genuine in every word. Her loud veracity sweeps through Fanny's dainty nothings like a salt sea breeze. And do not misunderstand the distinction. Fanny could not have told a lie to save her life. Mrs. Piozzi probably tossed them about like cherries or bonbons. But Mrs. Piozzi, laughing or lying, was always herself, without thinking about herself. Fanny was always thinking — unconsciously, if one may say so — of how she would appear to somebody else.

Thus I cannot agree with Mr. Dobson that her Diary is to be classed with the great diaries. A page of Pepys is enough to put her out of the count. She may be more decorous, more varied, even more entertaining. As a portrayer of her own soul or of the souls of others, between her and Pepys there is no comparison.

Take the mere matter of conversations. In these Miss Burney is inexhaustible. She gives an evening's talk of half a dozen personages, tricked out with the neatness of finished comic dialogue. She may keep the general drift of what was said. But who supposes her record can be exact? Exact enough, you say. In a sense, yes. Yet she turns humanity into literature. When Pepys quotes a sentence, you know you have the gross reality.

So, I repeat, our diarist helps us less than she ought. Yet even she cannot write two thousand pages, nominally about herself, without telling something. The very fact of such literary self-consciousness is of deep human interest. It is to be noted, also, that she does not conceal herself from any instinct of reserve. She is willing to drop pose and tell all, if she could; but she cannot. Such thoughtless self-confession as Pepys's would have been impossible to her. I do not think that once, in all her volumes, does she show herself in an unfavorable light.

But we can detect what she does not show. We can read much, much that she did not mean us to read. And lights are thrown on her by others as well as by herself.

To begin with, how did she bear glory? For a girl of twenty-five to be thrown into such a blaze of it was something of an ordeal. She herself disclaims any excessive ambition. She could almost wish the triumph might "happen to some other person who had more ambition, whose hopes were more sanguine, who could less have borne to be buried in the oblivion which I even sought." She records all the fine things that are said of her, the surmises of eager curiosity, the ardent outbursts of family affection, the really tumultuous enthusiasm of ripened critical judgment. But she is rather awed than inflated by it, at least, so she says. "I believe half the flattery I have had would have made me madly merry; but *all* serves only to depress me by the fulness of heart it occasions." "Steeped as she was in egotism," is the phrase used of her by Hayward, the biographer of Mrs. Piozzi. If she was so steeped, it certainly did not appear in outward obtrusiveness, pretense, or self-assertion. She repeatedly complains of her own shyness; and others, who knew her in very various surroundings, bear witness to it as strongly. "She was silent, backward, and timid, even to sheepishness," writes her father. "Dr. Burney and

his daughter, the author of 'Evelina' and 'Cecilia' . . .
I always thought rather avoided than solicited notice,"
says Wraxall. And Walpole, assuredly never inclined
to minimize defects, speaks with an enthusiasm which
is absolutely conclusive. Miss Burney "is half-and-half
sense and modesty, which possess her so entirely, that
not a cranny is left for pretense or affectation."

No. The author of "Evelina" may, must, have rev-
eled in the praise which was showered upon her in such
intoxicating measure. But she kept her head, and few
men or women ever lived who were less spoiled by flattery than she.

Indeed, her extreme shyness probably prevented her
being brilliantly successful in general society. She herself disposes summarily of her qualifications in this
regard. A hostess, she says, should provide for the
intellectual as well as the material wants of her guests.
"To take care of both, as every mistress of a table
ought to do, requires practice as well as spirits, and
ease as well as exertion. Of these four requisites I
possess not one."

This is the sort of thing one prefers saying one's self
to having others say it. There can be no doubt that
Miss Burney had tact, grace, charm, and above all,
that faculty of taking command of and saving a difficult situation which is one of the most essential of
social requisites. There is character in the pretty little
anecdote of her childhood. She and her playmates had
soaked and ruined a crusty neighbor's wig. He scolded.
For a while Fanny — ten years old — listened with
remorse and patience. Then she walked up to him and

said. "What signifies talking so much about an accident? The wig is wet, to be sure; and the wig was a good wig, to be sure; but 't is of no use to speak of it any more, because what's done can't be undone."

Still, she was doubtless at her best in companies of three or four friends, where she felt at her ease. She loved society and conversation, but it was of the intimate, fireside order. How fine is her remark on this point. "I determined, however, to avoid all tête-à-têtes with him whatsoever, as much as was in my power. How very few people are fit for them, nobody living in trios and quartettos can imagine!" She studied her interlocutors and adapted herself to them. "As soon as I found by the looks and expressions of this young lady, that she was of a peculiar cast, I left all choice of subjects to herself, determined quietly to follow as she led." She had also that charming gift for intimate society, the power — rather, the instinctive habit — of drawing confidences. Young and old, men and women, told her their hopes, their sorrows, their aspirations, and their difficulties. This, I think, does not commonly happen to persons steeped in egotism.

As it is delightful to turn from one trait in a character to another that seems quite incompatible with it, we must not assume that, because Miss Burney was shy and retiring, therefore she wanted spirits and gayety. On the contrary, she assures us, and the Diary and her other writings and her friends confirm it, that in good company she could carry laughter and hilarity to the pitch of riot. What a delicious picture does Crisp paint of her in childhood, dancing "Nancy Dawson on the grass-plot, with your cap on the ground, and your long hair streaming down your back, one shoe off, and throwing about your head like a mad thing." She was always ready to dance Nancy Dawson, and eager in sympathy when others danced. In the lively parts of "Evelina" there is a Bacchic boisterousness almost Rabelaisian, and again and again throughout the Diary scenes of pure, wild fun diversify the literary gravity of Streatham and the dull decorum of the court of George the Third.

But if Miss Burney could mock her friends, she could also love them, and to study her friendships is to study the woman herself. Mrs. Thrale-Piozzi does, indeed, write of her young protégée in rather harsh terms. Like all the rest of the Streatham world, Fanny was bitterly opposed to the Piozzi marriage, and her attitude provoked her former hostess to indignant criticism. Even in the earlier days of ardent affection, Mrs. Thrale notes some flaws in the relationship. Fanny was independent. Mrs. Thrale was patronizing. Fanny accepted favors a little as her due. Mrs. Thrale showered them, but wished them recognized. "Fanny Burney has kept her room here in my house seven days, with a fever or something that she calls a fever; I gave her every medicine and every slop with my own hand; took away her dirty cups, spoons, etc.; moved her tables; in short, was doctor, nurse, and maid — for I did not like the servants should have additional trouble, lest they should hate her for it. And now, with the true gratitude of a wit, she tells me that the world thinks the better of me for my civility to her. It does? does it?"

Can you not understand how Fanny felt? And how
Mrs. Thrale felt? And that they loved each other,
nevertheless, as Mrs. Thrale indeed eagerly admits?

Then came the Piozzi trouble and the lady speaks
harshly of "the treacherous Burneys." Yet I do not
think Fanny deserved it. She loved Dr. Johnson and
she loved Mrs. Thrale. Between them her course was
difficult. Also, she was undeniably conventional by
nature and Mrs. Thrale's irregularities shocked her.
Yet she did the best she could.

"Treacherous," said Mrs. Thrale. "True as gold,"
said Queen Charlotte. The latter is much nearer the
facts. Affection, loyal, devoted affection was the root
of Miss Burney's existence. She quotes Dr. Johnson's
saying to her, "Cling to those who cling to you," and I
am sure she was ready to carry it the one step further
which real loyalty requires. Her friends stick by her
and she by them. She defends them when they need it,
even when they hardly deserve it. "All else but kindness and society has to me always been nothing."

Especially charming is her devotion to her family.
The Memoirs of her father are three volumes of long
laudation. Almost equal is her affection for that singular figure, her other father, Samuel Crisp. Her sisters,
Susan especially, are loved and praised with like ecstasy and when her husband appears, her letters to him
and about him are as rapturous as was to be expected.
One exception to these family ardors stands out by its
oddity. Madame D'Arblay's only son is, in youth, not
what she would wish him to be — not dissipated, not
vicious, but unsocial, unconventional — and she ana-

lyzes him to his father with a critical coldness which, in her, is startling. "When he is wholly at his ease, as he is at present, . . . he is uncouth, negligent, and absent. . . . He exults rather than blushes in considering himself ignorant of everything that belongs to common life, and of everything that is deemed useful. . . . Sometimes he wishes for wealth, but it is only that he might be supine. . . . Yet, while thus open to every dupery, and professedly without any sense of order, he is so fearful of ridicule that a smile from his wife at any absurdity would fill him with the most gloomy indignation. It does so now from his mother." And thus we get sudden glimpses into deep gulfs of human nature, where it is hardly meant we should.

It seems almost an irony that a person of Miss Burney's social and conventional temper should have been forced into the excess of social convention — a court. She knew what was before her and hated it; for we like to indulge our failings in our own way. All the more, therefore, is one struck with the admirable qualities which such a trying experience calls out in her. To begin with, she maintains her dignity. Sensitive, shy, and timid as she was, it might be supposed that all court creatures would walk over her, from the king to the lowest lacquey, that in the busy struggle to climb she would be made a ladder-rung for every coarse or careless foot. No, it is clear she was not. She had no false pretensions, no whimsical assertion of pride in the wrong place. But she would not be imposed upon. How fine and straightforward is her statement of principle in the matter: "To submit to ill-humour rather than argue and dispute I think an exercise of patience, and I encourage myself all I can to practise it: but to accept even a shadow of an obligation upon such terms I should think mean and unworthy; and therefore I mean always, in a Court as I would elsewhere, to be open and fearless in declining such subjection."

Even finer is the force of character with which she resists depression and brooding over being torn from her friends and cut off from all her favorite pursuits. "Now therefore I took shame to myself and *resolved to be happy*." Happy she could not be, but such a resolution alters life, nevertheless, and shows an immense fund of character in the resolver. Similar resources she had shown before, when literary failure came to her as well as success. Accept the inevitable, resolutely control all thought of what cannot be helped, say nothing about it, and try something else. In short, she had a rich supply of that useful article, common sense. It is to be noted, also, that the heroines of her novels have it, for all their wild adventures.

With these various opportunities of human contact and with this natural shrewdness, Madame D'Arblay's Diary should have been a mine of varied and powerful observation of life. It is not. She presents us with a vast collection of figures, vividly contrasted and distinguished in external details and little personal peculiarities; but rarely, if ever, does she get down to essentials, to a real grip on the deeper springs and motives of character. This is in large part due to the eternal literary prepossession which I have already pointed out. You feel that the painter is much more interested in making an effective picture than a genuine likeness. But Miss Burney's deficiencies as an analyst of hearts go deeper than this technical artificiality and are bound up with one of the greatest charms of her personal temperament. For an exact observer of character she is altogether too amiable. I do not at all assert that a good student of men must hate them. Far from it.

> There is a soul of goodness in things evil,
> Would we observingly distil it out, —

is an excellent warning for the psychologist. But Miss Burney is really too full of the milk of human kindness. It oozes from every pore. She "tempers her satire with meekness," said Mrs. Thrale. She does indeed. Occasionally, in a very elaborate portrait, like that of her fellow courtier, Mr. Turbulent, she makes what the French call a *charge;* but even these are the rallying of joyous good-nature, not the bitter caricature of the born satirist. When, by rare chance, she does bring herself to a bitter touch, she usually atones for it by the observing distillation of a soul of goodness, which transfers the subject to the sheep category at once.

It is thus that her really vast gallery of portraiture is cruelly disappointing. Turn from her to Saint-Simon or Lord Hervey, turn even to the milder Greville or Madame de Rémusat, and you will feel the difference. George the Third was not Louis the Fourteenth, nor Queen Charlotte Queen Caroline. But George and his wife were hardly the beatific spirits that appear in this Diary. Miss Burney cannot say enough about her dear queen, her good queen, her saintly queen. Mrs. Thrale remarks: "The Queen's approaching death gives no concern but to the tradesmen, who want to sell their pinks and yellows, I suppose." And this is really refreshing after so much distillation of soul perfumery.

In short, though she was far from a fool, Miss Burney's views of humanity do more credit to her heart than to her head. If the paradox is permissible, she was exceedingly intelligent, but not very richly endowed with intelligence, that is, she was quick to perceive and reason in detail, but she had no turn for abstract thinking. The "puppy-men" at Bath complained to Mrs. Thrale that her young protégée had "such a drooping air and such a timid intelligence." This was greatly to the credit of the puppy-mens' discernment. Timid intellectually — not morally — Miss Burney certainly was. Such learning as she had she carefully disguised, and in this, no doubt, she had as fellows other eighteenth-century women much bigger than she. But when she gets hold of an attractive book, she waits to read it in company. "Anything highly beautiful I have almost an aversion to reading alone." Here I think we have a mark of social instincts altogether outbalancing the intellectual.

As to religious opinions, we have no right to criticize Miss Burney's reserve, because she tells us that it is of set purpose. At the same time it is noticeable how ready she is to look up to somebody else for her thinking. Her father, Crisp, Dr. Johnson, Mr. Locke, her husband, each in turn is an idol, a mainstay for the timid intelligence to cling to.

And as her intelligence was perhaps not Herculean, so I question whether her emotional life, just and tender and true as it indisputably was, had anything volcanic in it. She had certainly admirable control of her feelings; but in these cases we are never quite sure whether the force controlling is strong or the force controlled weak. Her love for her husband was rapturous — in words. Words were her stock in trade. It was also, no doubt, capable of supreme sacrifice; for her conscience was high and pure. Still, that "drooping air and timid intelligence" haunt me. She seems to approach all life, from God to her baby, with a delicious spiritual awe; so different from Miss Austen, who walks right up and lifts the veil of awe from everything. Miss Burney, indeed, stands as much in awe of herself as of everything else; and hence it is that, writing thousands of words about herself, she tells us comparatively little.

One thing is certain, she was a writer from her childhood to her death. Her own experiences and all others' were "copy," first and foremost. "I thought the lines *worth preserving;* so flew out of the room to write them." She was always flying out of life to preserve it — in syrup. The minute detail with which she writes out — or invents — all the conversations of her first love affair is extraordinary enough. Still, as she had no feeling in the matter herself, it was less wonderful that she could describe — not analyze — the young man's. But she did love her father. She did love her husband. That she could go from their deathbeds and note down last words and dying wishes, all the hopes and fears of those supreme moments, with cool artistic finish and posterity in her eye, is a fine instance of the scribbling mania.

MADAME D'ARBLAY

It is, therefore, as an authoress that we must chiefly think of her. It is as the fêted, flattered, worshiped creatress of "Evelina" that her girlish figure gets its finest piquancy; and she herself, in old age, must have gone back again and again, through all the varied agitations of fifty years, to that glorious evening when Johnson and Burke vied with each other in enthusiastic praise of her books, and as she left them, intoxicated with glory, Burke quietly said to her, "Miss Burney, die to-night."

V
MRS. PEPYS

CHRONOLOGY

Elizabeth Saint-Michel.
Born 1640.
Married Samuel Pepys December 1, 1655.
Died November 10, 1669.

Mrs. Pepys as St. Katharine

V

MRS. PEPYS

THE psychographer is apt to be hampered in his study of women by lack of material. Men of energy and vigor make themselves felt in the world at large. Even if they write little, they have a vast acquaintance, come into close contact with those who can write, and all their doings and sayings of importance are narrowly watched and minutely chronicled. In making their portraits one is more often embarrassed by the excess of material than by the lack of it.

With women this is not the case. Those who have public careers, historical figures, artists, writers especially, are approachable enough. And there is a great temptation to portray such mainly, if not exclusively. Yet so far from being all of the sex, they are not fairly representative of it, perhaps one may even say they are not normally representative. It is the quiet lives that count, the humble lives, the simple lives, lives perhaps of great achievement and of great influence, but of great influence through others, not direct. The richest and fullest and most fruitful of these lives often pass without leaving any written record, without a single trace that can be seized and followed to good purpose by the curious student. No doubt such women would prefer to be left in shadow, as they lived. But the loss to humanity in the study of their nobility and usefulness is very great. Above all, in portraying women of another type we should not forget these fugitive and silent figures who ought to be occupying the very first place in the history of their sex.

No one will maintain that Elizabeth, wife of Samuel Pepys, was an especially noble or heroic personage, or that her influence in the world, direct or indirect, was of a character to deserve any particular celebration. She appears, however, to have been thoroughly feminine and she is exceptional and interesting in this one point, at least, that she has not left posterity a single written line, yet she is known to us, from the Diary of her husband, with an intimacy and an accuracy of detail which we can hope to acquire with few characters who lived so long ago. George Sand remarked justly of Rousseau's "Confessions," that while he was without doubt at liberty to expose his own frailty, he had no right, in doing so, to expose the frailty of others. Right or wrong, Pepys certainly exposed his wife, in all her humanity, to the curious gaze of those who care to read. If we had a full volume of her letters, we could probably add something to certain phases of her experience, and more than anything else we should be glad to have her frank and daily comment on her husband. But, as it is, we know her as we know few of our living acquaintances and not all of our intimate friends.

When she first appears to us, she was twenty years old. Pepys married her at the early age of fifteen. It was a pure love match. He was poor and she was poor. Her father was a French Protestant. He was unsuccessful and unthrifty and Pepys helped the whole

family, so far as he could. Of Elizabeth's early life we
know little, except that her Catholic friends tried to
convert her. Of her married life before the Diary
begins, in 1660, we know nothing.

She was eminently beautiful. Pepys assures us of
that, and he was a connoisseur. Nor was this a lover's
illusion on his part. Years after his marriage, when too
much friction had set in between them, he reiterates his
opinion and notes with pride that she is not outdone by
the greatest beauties of the time: "My wife, by my
troth, appeared as pretty as any of them; I never
thought so much before; and so did Talbot and W.
Hewer, as they said, I heard, to one another." The
admiring husband does not attempt details, and perhaps it is as well. In the likenesses that have come
down to us we do not discern any singular charm: a
forehead rather full and prominent, eyebrows grace-
fully arched, a strongly marked nose, the mouth somewhat heavy, with lips, especially the upper, protruding.

That dress occupied a large place in Mrs. Pepys's
thoughts, as well as in her husband's finances, goes
without saying. He wishes her at all times to look well,
but is not always eager about paying the bills. She
follows the fashion, but not, it would seem, too curiously. Black patches, pendant curls, enhance, or dis-
figure, her natural charm. She cuts her dresses low in
the neck, considerably to Pepys's disgust, "out of a
belief, but without reason, that it is the fashion."
When worldly prospects are favorable, she gets gifts, —
for example, a new silk petticoat, "a very fine rich one,
the best I did see there, and much better than she de-

sires or expects." On the other hand, if a speculation — or a dinner — goes awry, her adornments are viewed less amiably. The purchase of a costly pair of earrings "did vex me and brought both me and her to very high and very foule words from her to me."

As this shows, she was in many ways a child; and what else should she have been? Married at fifteen, after a wandering and uncertain youth, how could she have attained solid training or any staid capacity? When she came to Pepys, she had apparently little education, but it is clear that she had a quick mother wit, so that with the passage of years she probably acquired as much as might decently justify the eulogy of her delightful epitaph, "*forma, artibus, linguis cultissima.*" Her husband was vexed by her false spelling, which must, therefore, have been indeed atrocious. But in his leisure hours he taught her arithmetic, geography, astronomy, and declares, in his patronizing way, that she made good profit.

She was a considerable reader, perhaps not of very solid literature, but at any rate of the poets and novelists. When obliged to remain at home, with a new Easter bonnet, on account of Pepys's indisposition, she consoles him, if not herself, by reading Fuller's "Worthies." On other similar occasions she reads Du Bartas or Ovid. Her erudition at times even produces a great effect on her husband, as when she assures him that the plot of a popular play is taken from a novel, goes home and puts the passage before him, also when she laboriously copies out a letter on jealousy from the "Arcadia" and submits it to him for his edification.

MRS. PEPYS

The romances that she loved she knew by heart, for her mentor finds occasion to check her for "her long stories out of Grand Cyrus, which she would tell, though nothing to the purpose, nor in any good manner."

When she was married, she had not many accomplishments. But Pepys wanted a wife who would do him credit and took pains to teach her. Also, it must be added that music was one of the greatest pleasures of his life and he tried hard to share it with her. Sometimes he is encouraged. She really has quite a voice, if it were not that she has no ear. And even if she has no voice, she is so deft with her fingers that he is sure she will play the flageolet charmingly. Then it ends too often in the wail of the musical temperament over the temperament that is not musical and never can be. With drawing it is somewhat better. The lady makes progress; she decidedly outdoes Peg Penn, which is gratifying, and in one case, at least, her husband defers abjectly to her esthetic judgment. I "did choose two pictures to hang up in my house, which my wife did not like when I came home, and so I sent the picture of Paris back again."

Mrs. Pepys's enthusiasm for her artistic pursuits was so great as occasionally to bring reproach upon her for neglect of her household duties. But in general we may conclude that she was a faithful, a devoted, and an interested housekeeper. In a girl of twenty some slips were surely to be expected. "Finding my wife's clothes lie carelessly laid up, I was angry with her, which I was troubled for." The record, however, usually indicates both intelligence and energy. "My poor wife, who

95

works all day at home like a horse," remarks the not always appreciative husband. There are spurts of cleanliness, when the lady and her maids rise early and labor late, with a grim determination to rid their belongings of dirt, that monster of the world. Every woman will sympathize and will resent the unkindly comment of the observing cynic: "She now pretends to a resolution of being hereafter very clean. How long it will hold I can guess."

Washing seems to have been done with a thoroughness which makes up for its rarity. Washing day upsets the whole household and with it Mr. Pepys's temper, because he had invited friends to dinner and did not see how preparations could possibly be made to receive them. Nevertheless, I imagine the guests were received, and had no suspicions. A good housewife can work those miracles. At another time he goes to bed late and leaves mistress and maids still washing, washing.

The lady was a cook, too, and no doubt a good one. Many a dinner of her getting is minutely detailed and many more of her supervising. As has happened to others, her new oven bakes too quickly and burns her tarts and pies, but she "knows how to do better another time." And this is a little touch of character, is it not?

But the sweetest picture of Mrs. Pepys at work is drawn by her husband's memory, as he looks back from growing fortune on cottage days and simple love. "Talking with pleasure with my poor wife, how she used to make coal fires, and wash my foul clothes with her own hand for me, poor wretch! in our little room at my Lord Sandwich's; for which I ought for ever to love and admire her, and do; and persuade myself she would do the same thing again, if God should reduce us to it."

Riches diminish some cares and swell others. In the little room at Lord Sandwich's the servant problem was not serious. Afterwards it became so. A procession of sweet old English names, Nells and Janes and Nans and Debs, gleams and dances through the Diary, sometimes in tears, sometimes in laughter, sometimes trim, dainty, and coquettish, sometimes red-armed and tousle-headed. Some please master and mistress both, some please only the mistress, some, alas! — not the red arms and tousled heads — please only the master and fill that quaint and ancient Pepysian domesticity with tragedy and woe. Nothing, absolutely nothing, not even her children, tests a woman's character so much as do her servants. From all that we read, it seems safe to assume that Mrs. Pepys showed judgment, common sense, and balance in the treatment of hers. If she flew out occasionally, we must remember that she was very young and that she lived with servants in very close intimacy. I fancy that her voice had deserved weight in the pretty little scene which took place in the garden and the moonlight. "Then it being fine moonshine with my wife an houre in the garden, talking of her clothes against Easter and about her mayds, Jane being to be gone, and the great dispute whether Besse, whom we both love, should be raised to be chamber-mayde or no. We have both a mind to it, but know not whether we should venture the making her proud and so make a bad chamber-mayde of a good-natured and sufficient cook-mayde."

Probably the greatest wrecker of domestic peace is and always has been money. Was Mrs. Pepys a good economist? She was woman enough, human enough, to take delight in comfort and luxury. A new hanging, a new picture, a new bit of furniture enchanted her, as did a frock or a jewel. The purchase of the family coach was a matter of manifest rejoicing. Also, she was not perfect in her accounts, and when called to a stern audit by her source of supply, was forced to admit that she sometimes juggled with the figures, a confession truly horrible to one whose Philistine morality strained at a commercial gnat and swallowed a sexual camel. It "madded me and do still trouble me, for I fear she will forget by degrees the way of living cheap and under sense of want." Nevertheless, her management is usually approved. After all, she costs less than other wives, a good many; and occasions of expense for her are not so frequent, all things considered. Even, in one felicitous instance, she receives praise, of that moderate sort which must often content the starved susceptibilities of matrimony. "She continuing with the same care and thrift and innocence, so long as I keep her from occasions of being otherwise, as ever she was in her life."

One question that occurs frequently in regard to Mrs. Pepys is, had she friends? Apparently she had none. Perhaps her vague and troubled youth had kept her from contracting any of the rapturous intimacies of girlhood. If she had done so, they did not survive marriage. For Pepys was not the man to let his wife's close companions pass without comment. He would have hated them — or loved them, and in either case made his house not over-pleasant to them. Perhaps he had done so before the Diary begins. At any rate, while Mrs. Pepys had many acquaintances, we do not see that she had one real confidante to whom she entrusted the many secrets that she obviously had to entrust. And in consequence she was lonely. The Diary shows it in touching fashion. Pepys recognizes it, but, with a certain cold-bloodedness, prefers having her lonely at home to having her dissipated abroad. So she is left to gossip and bicker with her maids, to pet her dogs and birds, and to quarrel with her husband. Even of her own family she sees little. Pepys did not seek their company, because they always wanted something. And they did not seek his, because they did not always get what they wanted, though with them, as with others, he was usually just and often generous.

It must not, however, be supposed that Mrs. Pepys was a Cinderella, or that the maids in the kitchen were her sole society. Pepys was proud of her, proud of his house, proud of his hospitality, which enlarged as riches came. He took her about with him often to the houses of his friends. Now and again they made a journey together with great peace of mind and curious content. Also, few weeks passed that he did not bring some one home with him, for dancing, or music, or general merriment, and in all these doings Mrs. Pepys's share was greater or less. I think we can easily surmise her hand in that royal and triumphant festivity, the mere narrative of which breeds joy as well as laughter in any well-tempered disposition. "We fell to dancing, and continued, only with intermission for a good supper, till two in the morning, the music being Greeting, and another most excellent violin, and theorbo, the best in town. And so with mighty mirth, and pleased with their dancing of jigs afterwards several of them, and among others, Betty Turner, who did it mighty prettily; and, lastly, W. Batelier's 'Blackmore and Blackmore Mad'; and then to a country-dance again, and so broke up with extraordinary pleasure, as being one of the days and nights of my life spent with the greatest content; and that which I can but hope to repeat again a few times in my whole life. This done, we parted, the strangers home, and I did lodge my cozen Pepys and his wife in our blue chamber. My cozen Turner, her sister, and The., in our best chamber; Bab., Betty, and Betty Turner in our own chamber; and myself and my wife in the maid's bed, which is very good. Our maids in the coachman's bed; the coachman with the boy in his settle-bed, and Tom where he uses to lie. And so I did, to my great content, lodge at once in my house, with the greatest ease, fifteen, and eight of them strangers of quality." And surely Mrs. Pepys was the queen of the feast, even though her name is but once mentioned.

Moreover, she had the social instinct, and gave her husband advice as to his conduct in the world, which he himself recognizes as excellent, and resolves to follow it. "I told all this day's passages, and she to give me very good and rational advice how to behave myself to my Lord and his family, by slighting everybody but my Lord and Lady, and not to seem to have the least society or fellowship with them, which I am resolved to do, knowing that it is my high carriage that must do me good there, and to appear in good clothes and garbe."

In one of Pepys's diversions, which meant more to him than any except, perhaps, music, Mrs. Pepys was allowed to share to a considerable extent, and that was theatre-going. It would seem that she entered into it almost as heartily as did her husband and with quite as intelligent criticism. In one of his delightful spells of conscience-ache, he reproaches himself for going to a play alone, after swearing to his wife that he would go no more without her. But he sometimes permits her to go alone and very often enjoys her company and her enthusiasm. Occasionally she differs from him without shaking his judgment. But they agree entirely in their delight in Massinger's "*Bondman*" and as entirely in their contempt for "*A Midsummer Night's Dream.*"

When one considers the frailties that resulted from Pepys's social relations, one is tempted to ask how Mrs. Pepys was affected in this regard. So far as we can judge, it was not an age of very nice morality, at any rate among the upper classes. Wives as fair and as respectable as Pepys's seem to have entertained the addresses of lovers more or less numerous. But I think we may assume that the lady we are concerned with was all that a wife should be. Pepys himself was undoubtedly of that opinion and he was an acute and a by no means partial judge. He does, indeed, have tempestuous bursts of jealousy. There was a certain dancing master,

Pembleton by name, who caused a great deal of uneasiness. It is pretty evident that Mrs. Pepys coquetted with him, perhaps intentionally, and drove her husband at times to the verge of frenzy, perhaps intentionally. It "do so trouble me that I know not at this very minute that I now write this almost what either I write or am doing." But it blows over with the clear admission that the parties had been nothing more than indiscreet.

Also, I divine a little malice in that pleasant incident of later date, when Mrs. Pepys appears with a couple of fine lace pinners, at first causing infinite disquiet by the suspicion that they were a present and then dispelling this disagreeable state of mind by another hardly less disagreeable. "On the contrary, I find she hath bought them for me to pay for them, without my knowledge."

Under other aspects of morality, Mrs. Pepys perhaps impresses us less favorably. She would seem to have had faults of temper, faults of tongue, to be at times inclined to deception, at times to violence. Here again her age must be remembered, her age and her training. I imagine that in some moral points she was more practical than her husband, less inclined to hair-splitting nicety. I would give a good deal to know what she thought of his precious business of vows, his fine distinctions as to indulgence and abstinence, his forfeits, his pretexts and subterfuges. When he made up for a vow broken in an extra visit to the theatre by getting her to substitute one of her visits which she could not use, I can see her soothing agreement, "Oh, yes, Sam, of course, why not?" And I can see also the fine smile twitching the corners of her pretty mouth as she watched the departing Phariseeism of those sturdy English shoulders.

What religion she had back of her morals — or immorals — we do not know. Although, in the enthusiasm of first love, she announced that she had a husband who would help her out of popery, she doubtless soon found that there was not much spiritual comfort to be had from one who in good fortune boasted of sharing the utter irreligion of Lord Sandwich and, when things went wrong, dreaded abjectly that the Lord God would punish him for his sins. Curious depths of inward experience suggest themselves from the fact that Mrs. Pepys became a Catholic and received the sacrament, without a single suspicion on the part of her watchful inquisitor. Yet, after all, there may have been little spiritual experience, but merely a deft confessor and an unresponsive world.

So it is hard to find out whether Mrs. Pepys loved God and it is equally hard to find out what we are even more eager to know, whether she loved her husband. In considering the point, we must remember first that the world saw him quite other than we see him in the Diary. We see the lining of his soul, somewhat spotted and patched and threadbare. The world at large saw the outer tissue which was really imposing and magnificent. Not only was he a useful, prosperous, successful public servant and man of business, but he had more than the respect, the esteem and admiration, of the best men of his time, as a scholar and a gentleman. Here, therefore, was a husband to be proud of.

Pride does not make love, however. And we know well that folly and even vice often hold a woman's heart closer and longer than well-laundered respectability. It would appear that Mr. Pepys might have combined all the desired qualifications with peculiar success. Yet as to the result, I repeat, we do not know. And it is strange that we do not. Every shade of the husband's varying feelings is revealed to us, but what the wife felt he does not record, because, alas, he does not greatly care. Or, rather, may we say that he assumed that she worshiped him? And may we not go further and conclude that he was right in so assuming and that for one word of real affection she was ready to lay all her whims and errors and vagaries at his feet? Is not this attitude quite compatible with understanding him completely?

His family she did not love, nor they her. The case is not unprecedented. Very likely she tried her best. Very likely they tried their best. But she was young and fashionable and quick-witted. They were old, some of them, and all of them antique. Then they adored Sam, who was making the family. Well, so did she. But she knew Sam and did not care to have his Sunday attitudes and platitudes thrust upon her perpetually.

If they had only had children, how different it might all have been! Pepys as a father would have furnished one more delight to the civilized world. Mrs. Pepys as a mother would have come in for some bad half hours, but she would have been more cherished and even more interesting. There is little evidence that Pepys regretted his childless state, or that his wife did. But we can guess how it was with her.

I have said that Pepys's feelings towards his wife can be seen in minute detail all through the Diary. The study of them is profoundly curious. That he was an ardent lover before marriage is manifest from many casual observations, notably from one of the most high-wrought and passionate entries in the entire record. "But that which did please me beyond anything in the whole world was the wind-musique when the angel comes down, which is so sweet that it ravished me, and indeed, in a word, did wrap up my soul so that it made me really sick, just as I have formerly been when in love with my wife."

The calm daylight of matrimonial domesticity paled these raptures to a very considerable extent. It has done so in other cases. The dull wear of duns and debts, the friction of household management, an ill-cooked dinner, an ill-dusted study — these things may not shatter the foundations of love, but they do a little tarnish its fresh trim and new felicity. Yet, though the husband is no longer made "almost sick" by the lover's rapturous longing, there are plenty of instances of a solid habit of affection, growing firmer and more enduring with the passage of years. When she is away on a visit, his heart is heavy for the absence of his dear wife, all things seem melancholy without her, and he is filled with satisfaction at her return. When she is ill, suddenly and violently ill, his anxiety and distress prove to him his great love for her, though, when the crisis is past, his incomparable candor adds, "God forgive me!

I did find that I was most desirous to take my rest than to ease her, but there was nothing I could do to do her any good with." When the world goes wrong and life seems nothing but toil and trouble, he turns to her and gets her to comfort him.

It is true that that relentless Diary has scenes as painful as they are curious, scenes in which the estimable naval secretary and friend of Newton and Evelyn comports himself after a fashion that would be disgraceful in any station of life. There are outbursts of jealousy and fits of temper, kickings of furniture and trinkets smashed in spite, abuse, blows, and nose and ear pullings of intolerable indignity. The fault is confessed and temporarily forgotten, "Last night I was very angry, and do think I did give her as much cause to be angry with me." Then, some wretched trifle, an ill-timed visit, a shilling mis-spent, a foolish fashion followed, sets all awry again. I do not know where in literature to find a fiercer or more cutting scene of domestic infelicity than that of the tearing of the old love letters. Mrs. Pepys had written a remonstrance as to some phases of ill-treatment. "She now read it, and it was so piquant, and wrote in English, and most of it true, of the retiredness of her life, and how unpleasant it was; that being wrote in English, and so in danger of being met with and read by others, I was vexed at it, and desired her and then commanded her to tear it: when she desired to be excused, I forced it from her, and tore it, and withal took her other bundle of papers from her. . . . I pulled them out one by one and tore them all before her face, though it went against my heart to do it, she crying and desiring me not to do it, but such was my passion and trouble to see the letters of my love to her . . . to be joyned with a paper of so much disgrace to me and dishonour, if it should have been found by anybody."

Things like this, one would say, could never be forgotten. Yet they are. "After winter comes summer," says the "Imitation," "after the night the day, and after a storm a great calm." Great calms came in the Pepys family also. "I home, and to writing, and heare my boy play on the lute, and a turne with my wife pleasantly in the garden by moonshine, my heart being in great peace, and so home to supper and to bed." Truly, life is made up of delightful — and pitiful — contrasts.

The worst domestic troubles of the Pepyses were caused by the husband's extreme susceptibility to feminine charm. "A strange slavery that I stand in to beauty," he remarks, with that pleased amazement at himself which makes him so attractive.

The detail of these infatuations — how they were mildly resisted at first, and how they grew and developed to an extent hardly possible for such a man in a less scandalous age, how they were indulged, and then repented, and again indulged, and again repented — belongs to the history of Mr. Pepys — and of human nature. Mrs. Pepys knew little of them, though she divined much.

What does concern her is the very instructive fashion in which she gradually gained power over her husband by his infidelities themselves. She knew well that he loved her at heart. At any rate, she knew that he was tied to her by bonds of habit and circumstance which a man of his temperament could never shake off. Therefore, by the aid of jealousy and tears and scenes she learned that she could in time mould him to almost anything she wished. This experience begins with outsiders, with Mrs. Pierce and Mrs. Knipp. A little well-placed anger — certainly not feigned — was found to accomplish wonders. "Which is pretty to see how my wife is come to convention with me, that whatever I do give to anybody else, I shall give her as much, which I am not much displeased with." By the time the crisis of the maid, Deb Willett, had arrived, Mrs. Pepys had become past-mistress in the art of working on her husband's sensibilities. Note that I do not mean that this was a coldly deliberate process; simply, that all the instinct of her outraged affection concentrated itself on energetic means of overcoming this foolish and recalcitrant male, and triumphed magnificently. Deb is wooed and forsaken and wooed again and banished. The man's will is bent, and bent, and bent, till he comes right square down upon his knees: "Therefore I do, by the grace of God, promise never to offend her more, and did this night begin to pray to God upon my knees alone in my chamber, which God knows I cannot yet do heartily; but I hope God will give me the grace more and more every day to fear Him, and to be true to my poor wife."

Even after this the symptoms recur, but milder, and in that pathetic blank stop which ends the Diary because of failing sight, the phrase "my amours to Deb are past," seems to leave the wife victorious, we hope permanently.

So, after we have known her for nine years in the closest intimacy, she steps out from us into great night. A few months later, still a young woman, she died; but she dies for us with the last line of her husband's imperishable record. In that record it may be said, in a certain sense, that she is shown at the greatest possible disadvantage, as we may in part realize, if we consider what a similar record would have been, kept by herself. Yet even seen as her husband reports her, we feel that she had, with much of a woman's weakness, much also of a woman's charm.

VI
Madame de Sévigné

CHRONOLOGY

Marie de Rabutin-Chantal.
Born 1626.
Married Marquis de Sévigné 1644.
Husband died 1651.
Died 1696.

Madame de Sévigné

VI

MADAME DE SÉVIGNÉ

MERELY as a literary figure, as a writer, Madame de Sévigné amply justifies her claim to celebrity in the greatest age of French letters. As a mistress of style she is the worthy contemporary of Molière, Corneille, Pascal, and La Fontaine.

Yet she wrote only letters and wrote those letters as naturally as she talked. Just before her came Balzac and Voiture, who wrote epistles, after the fashion of Pliny and James Howell. Now, Madame de Sévigné knows that she writes well and takes pride in it, just as Cicero did; but like him, she knows that letters, to be of any interest, must be sincere, must be written for matter, not manner. Hers flow from her heart direct, as she says; they pour forth all the passion, the curiosity, the laughter of the moment. Often she does not even reread them before sending. The far-fetched felicities of a laborious writer fill her with disgust. Of the style of one such she writes, "It is insupportable to me. I had rather be coarse than be like her. She drives me to forget delicacy, refinement, and politeness, for fear of falling into her juggler's tricks. Now is n't it sad to become just a mere peasant?"

Peasant or not, she makes the whole wide world of the French seventeenth century live in her letters, as does Saint-Simon, in his Memoirs, somewhat later; and in Madame de Sévigné it lives more vividly, if in Saint-Simon more profoundly. The great affairs of princes and their petty humanness, the splendor of war and its hideous cruelty, intrigues of courtiers, intrigues of lovers, new books, new plays, new prayers, fashion, folly, tears, and laughter, all mingle in her pages and help us understand to-day and to-morrow by their deep and startling similitude with yesterday. As "human documents" these letters have rarely been surpassed.

But the most interesting thing in her letters is her soul, and she lays bare every fold and fibre of it, without the slightest bravado of self-revelation, but also without any attempt at reserve or concealment. She defies our minutest curiosity, because she could.

Above all, she was a healthy, normal temperament, with all the elements delightfully blended, a rich, human creature of balance and sanity. She knew well that life is of a mingled yarn, at its best not free from bitterness. She knew well what passion is, what grief is. This is just what makes her so rounded and so human. But, in most things, she held a sure rein and kept her heart in reasonable harmony with her intelligence.

As a practical manager she was admirable. Her husband, who fortunately died early, was a spendthrift. So was her son, and her daughter not much better. But the wife and mother knew the excellent utility of money, watched carefully her great estate, scolded her agents, spent largely when she could, and when she could not, went without. She accuses herself of avarice, as the avaricious never do. But we know that she was prudent, and forethoughtful, and discreet.

MADAME DE SÉVIGNÉ

I am sure, also, that she was perfect mistress of her
household. But it is a strange thing that a woman,
writing a thousand of the frankest long letters, should
say scarcely a word about her servants. Could you
imitate her, madam? And do you not agree with me
that it is an indication of strong sense and native tact?

Let us trace further the charming many-sidedness
of this beautifully rounded character. She was a
Parisian, a child of brick and mortar, her ears well
tuned to the hubbub of city streets, yet she loved the
country, not for hasty week-ends of dress and gossip,
but for its real quiet and solitude. She felt its melancholy. "In these woods reveries sometimes fall upon
me so black that I come out of them as if I had had
a touch of fever." And when she rambles under the
shade of melancholy boughs, with Madame de La
Fayette and La Rochefoucauld, whose company one
would not have supposed exhilarating, their conversations are "so dismal that you would think there was
nothing else to do but bury us." Yet the quick, sweet
reaction of her sunny temper shows in the very next
sentence. "Madame de La Fayette's garden is the loveliest thing in the world. It is all flowers, all sweetness."

She herself assures her friends that they need not
fear that country solitude will bore her and make her
morbid. "Except for pangs of heart, against which I
am too weak, there is nothing to pity me for. I am
naturally happy and get on with everything and am
amused with everything." So, if the song of a nightingale could fill her eyes with tears, in another instant,
like the merry Phædria, she could "laugh at shaking of

the leavés light." It is she who invented that exquisite spring phrase, "the singing woods," she who calls herself "lonely as a violet, easy to be hid," she who knows the love of mute insensate things, "I understand better than any one in the world the sort of attachment one has for inanimate objects." How fresh and charming is the picture of her wading in the morning dew up to her knees to take an eager survey of her open-air possessions.

With that other joy of solitude, books, she is as engaging and as frank as with the natural world. It would be absurd to think of her as a pedant, or a bluestocking. Any call of the normal feminine pursuits of life found her quickly and readily responsive, her best books cast into a corner, forgotten. Yet she did love them. "When I step into this library, I cannot understand why I ever step out of it." She can pass long hours wholly absorbed in new authors, or old ones. Her comments on the great French literature that was springing up about her are always fresh, shrewd, and suggestive. Of Racine's religious plays she says, "Racine has outdone himself; he loves God as he loved his mistresses; he enters into sacred things as he did into profane." La Fontaine she prized as one born under the same planet. He was gay like her, tender like her, loved the birds and flowers like her, and like her, kept his tears in the closest contact with his laughter. I feel a certain yearning in the words with which she socially condemns the wayward poet. "You can only thank God for such a man and pray to have nothing to do with him."

MADAME DE SÉVIGNÉ

But novels, novels! Assuredly no one ever loved them more than Madame de Sévigné, those interminable ten-volume romances of chivalry and sentiment which she pored over, as later generations pored over Richardson, or Scott, or Dumas, or Victor Hugo. No one has ever expressed more vivaciously than she the fascination we feel in these books, even when our cooler judgment laughs at them: "The style of La Calprenède is wretched in a thousand places: the swelling romantic phrases, the ill-assorted words, I feel them all. I admit that such language is detestable, and all the time the book holds me like glue. The beauty of the sentiments, the violence of the passions, the great scale of the incidents, and the miraculous success of the hero's redoubtable sword — it sweeps me away as if I were a girl again."

Yet though she could make such rich and ample use of the resources of nature and books in solitude, she was the last person in the world to shrink from human society. As a friend she was exquisite. She practised friendship widely, yet discreetly, as one of the most delicious arts of life. "I am nice in my friendships and it is a business in which I am sufficiently expert." She recognized those whom she felt to be akin to her, even when she knew them but by hearsay, and she mourns over the death of a friend's friend because she loved her, though, she says, "only by reverberation."

She had friends of both sexes and all kinds. She was devoted alike to the magnificent Fouquet, the gay, volatile, and malicious Bussy, the brilliant, ardent Retz, the cynical La Rochefoucauld, the wise and quiet scholar, Corbinelli. It is difficult to say whether she loved most the grave, thoughtful, sentimental Madame de La Fayette, or Madame de Coulanges with whom she could play the lightest, daintiest sort of epistolary battledore and shuttlecock. So souls were honest and right-minded and of stuff to knit loyally with hers, they were all acceptable to her.

For she was beautifully, nobly, femininely loyal in all these different friendships. Perhaps the best known of her letters are those in which she relates the trial of Fouquet on charges of maladministration in his great financial office. With what passionate eagerness does she narrate every detail from day to day, the judges' malevolence (as she views it), the varying testimony, the gradual approach of doom, and above all, the lofty, admirable bearing of the accused! With what indignant grief does she resent and resist — in spirit — the conviction and the punishment. And in lesser troubles she has the same firm fidelity. Contagious illness, what is that in a matter of friendship? "I feel about infections as you do about precipices, there are people with whom I have no fear of them." Disagreements, controversies, quarrels? —

> "To be wroth with one we love
> Doth work like madness in the brain." —

"In our family," she says, of one such, "we do not lose affection. The bonds may stretch, but they never break." And again, when she is hurt by coldness and indifference, she protests, "Ah, how easy it really is to live with me! A little gentleness, a little social impulse, a little confidence, even superficial, will lead me such a long way. I do believe that no one is more responsive than I in the daily intercourse of life."

Yet, though she had many friends and loved them, it must not be supposed that she was love-blinded or without keen insight into folly and weakness. She was a careful observer of the facts of human nature, and could say with Pepys, whom she resembles in some points, not in others, "I confess that I am in all things curious." Indeed, she herself remarks of one who had died in a rather unusual manner, "I perfectly understand your desire to see her. I should like to have been there myself. I love everything that is out of the common." And a sympathetic acquaintance writes, after Madame de Sévigné's own death: "You appear to have the taste of your late friend, who yearned for details and baptized them as 'the style of friendship.'"

One who looked so closely into souls, and especially one who was a near friend of La Rochefoucauld, could not escape some harsh conclusions, could not avoid seeing that all is not love that speaks kindly, nor all honor that pranks itself in stately phrase. Madame de Sévigné had her moments when she lost faith in humanity, moments of despair, moments of still more melancholy mocking. When she is most touched with the spirit of her cynical associate, she writes, "We like so much to hear people talk of us and of our motives, that we are charmed even when they abuse us." And again, "The desire to be singular and to astonish by ways out of the common seems to me to be the source of many virtues." One day, when she was especially out of sorts, she let her quick wit amuse itself

imagining what it would be to take the roof off of too
many households that she knew and see inside the hate,
the jealousy, the bickering, the pettiness that are
veiled so carefully under the decorous fashions of the
world.

Nevertheless, it would be wholly unjust to class her
with La Rochefoucauld or with any one who was a
cynic by permanent habit of thought. She observed
men and women because she loved them. She knew
that their faults were her faults and that what was good
in her was to be found in them also. In no one is more
obvious and unfailing the large spirit of tolerance and
charity so exquisitely expressed by old Fagon, physician to King Louis the Fourteenth, "*Il faut beaucoup
pardonner à la nature.*" It is true that her native spirit
of merriment cannot resist a good joke, however it
comes. "Friendship," she says, "bids us be indignant
with those who speak against our friends; but it does
not forbid us to be amused when they speak wittily."
Yet she had always and everywhere that deepest and
most essential element of human kindness, the faculty
of putting herself in another's place, and her sense of
the laughable in trivial misfortunes was not so keen as
her ready and active sympathy in great.

Therefore she was popular and widely beloved and
largely sought after. In her youth and even in her later
maturity she was beautiful. Precisely because her
beauty was less of the features than of the expression,
it lasted longer than mere pink cheeks and delicate
contours. Her soul laughed in her eyes and her merry
and fortunate thoughts spoke as much in her gestures

and the carriage of her body as in the quick grace of her
Parisian tongue. And though no human being was less
vain, she no doubt knew her charm, and prized it, and
cultivated it in all due and proper ways. "There is
nothing so lovely as to be beautiful. Beauty is a gift of
God and we should cherish it as such."

Delicious is the word her friends most often use of
her. "Your letters are delicious and so are you," writes
one of them. "She was delicious to live with," said
another. And her son-in-law, with whom she had sharp
spats at times, yet declared that "delicious" was the
true name for her society.

The fact is, she loved to be with men and women,
and therefore they loved to be with her. Being flesh
and blood, she sometimes tired of the invitations and
festivities that were thrust upon her. There were recep-
tions and entertainments without end, court functions
and private functions. "I wish with all my soul I were
out of here where they honor me too much. I am hun-
gry for privation and silence." And again, when the
courtesies rained as thickly as blossoms in May, and
tired nerves rebelled against late eating sauced with
interminable chatter, "When, when can I die of hunger
and keep still?" Also, being a creature of petulant wit,
she could not fail occasionally to find average humanity
— that is, you and me — somewhat tedious.

Yet she makes the best, even of such tediousness, in
her kindly, human way, and turns it into gentle pleas-
antry. After all, she argues, it is much better to mix
with bad company than good. Why? Because when
the bad leaves you, you are not a bit sorry. But parting

with those whose society is delightful leaves you utterly at a loss how to resume the common life of every day. Does not this last touch of hers recall many a poignant minute of your own? This is 'what makes Madame de Sévigné so charming, that in giving perfect expression to every shade of her feeling she is finding immortal utterance for your feelings and for mine. "Sometimes I am seized with the fancy to cry at a great ball, and sometimes I give way to my fancy, without any one's ever knowing it."

Crying or laughing, she went to balls and banquets, and enjoyed them, and described them with the golden glow of her decorative imagination. "I went to the marriage of Mademoiselle de Louvois. What shall I say about it? Magnificence, gorgeousness, all France, garments loaded and slashed with gold, jewels, a blaze of fires and flowers, a jam of coaches, cries in the street, torches flaring, poor folk thrust back and run over; in short, the usual whirlwind of nothing, questions not answered, compliments not meant, civilities addressed to no one in particular, everybody's feet tangled up in everybody's train." And she went home weary and resolved not to go again. And she went again — like all of us.

It will naturally be asked whether, in an age of too courtly morals, when exact virtue was not always insisted upon, perhaps not even expected, this gay young widow lived within the limits of propriety. It can only be said that the keenest scandal-mongers of the time — and none were ever keener — find no fault with her in this respect. She had passionate lovers of all sorts,

princes, generals, statesmen, poets. She laughed with
them all, picked the fine flower of their adoration, and
went on her way untouched, so far as it appears. What
the passions were she knew well, as is shown clearly
enough in the wonderful sentence in which she com-
pares them to vipers, which may be bruised and
crushed and torn and trampled, and still they move;
you may tear their hearts out, and still they move.
But for her own, she flourished in spite of them, not
perhaps with white innocence, but with royal self-
possession.

And this self-possession was not wholly the outcome
of coldness, nor even of balanced sanity. A large
amount of spiritual elevation entered into it, a religious
fervor which, if not always haunting, is rarely far away.
Madame de Sévigné took nice and constant counsel for
the welfare of her soul. With all her ample sense of the
charm and solace of this world, she was very much
alive to the awful immanence of another. Time flies,
she says, "and I see it fly with horror, bringing me
hideous old age, disease, and death." Again, "I find
death so terrible, that I hate life more because it brings
me to it than because of the thorns that strew the
path." She assuages the horror with devout practice.
On suitable occasions she resolves to withdraw from
the world, pray and fast much, and "practice boredom for the love of God." She is a faithful and constant reader of the fathers and the moralists. She
listens to the great sermons of Bossuet and Bordaloue,
and profits, though her shrewd wit is sometimes critical. Above all, she strives for a humble, earnest atti-

tude of submission to the will of God everywhere and
always. Without this, she thinks, life would be unbear-
able. The sense of His presence and of His guidance,
the solution of sin and suffering by His all-controlling
and all-loving will are never far from her. At moments
she even rises to something of the mystic's joy.

Yet she was no mystic, but in this aspect of life also a
sane and normal woman, and it is delicious, because so
human, to see how the pressure of this world returns
upon her and crowds out even God. How charming is
her naïve report of the verdict of a suggested confessor.
"I have seen the Abbé de la Vergne; we talked about
my soul; he says that unless he can lock me up, not stir
a step from me, take me to and from church himself,
and neither let me read, speak, nor hear a single thing,
he will have nothing to do with me whatever." The
saints, the saints! She envies them, of course. But
they are so dowdy. The sinners are so much more
agreeable. And the ways of this world are pleasant,
pleasant. Dark thoughts, dark hours will intrude, will
overcome us like a summer cloud, and then we get out
Pascal or Nicole and hurry to the altar. But who can
live on this level long? Yes, she is mean and low and
base, she says. When she sees people too happy it fills
her with despair, which is not the fashion of a beautiful
soul. She is not a beautiful soul, calls herself a soul of
mud. How can any prayer, or any religion, or any God
save her?

She has her moments, also, not of defiance, but of
question whether it is worth while to make one's self
unhappy. "You must love my weaknesses, my faults,"

she says. "For my part I put up with them well enough." After all, if she is lukewarm, and easy-going, and forgetful, so are others, millions of others. Why should she suffer for it more than they? We practice salvation with the saints, she says, and damnation with the children of this world. "We are not the devil's," she says, "because we fear God and because at bottom we have a touch of religion. We are not God's, either, because His law is hard and we do not wish to do ourselves a damage. This is the state of the lukewarm, and the great number of them does not disturb me. I enter perfectly into their reasons. At the same time God hates them and they ought to escape from their condition; but this is precisely the difficulty."

No one has portrayed more exquisitely than she the pitiful but human lightness of common souls in face of these enormous questions. "My saintly friend sometimes finds me as reasonable and serious as she would have me. And then, a whiff of spring air, a ray of sunshine, sweeps away all the reflections of the twilight gloom." And it is she who framed the advice, dangerous or precious according to the heart it falls on. "*Il faut glisser sur les pensées et ne pas les approfondir.*" It is sometimes best to slip over thoughts and not go to the bottom of them.

So we have seen Madame de Sévigné to be in every respect a sweetly rounded nature, one of the most so, one of the most sane, normal, human women that have left the record of their souls for the careful study of posterity. Well, in this pure and perfect crystal of balanced common sense and judgment there was one most curious and interesting flaw, the lady's love for her daughter. Love for her daughter? you repeat. And is not that the most sane and normal of all possible characteristics in a woman?

It ought to be. But in Madame de Sévigné it certainly was not. She had two children, a daughter and a son. The son much resembled her, with some of her good qualities exaggerated into faults. He was gay and kindly; but he was light-headed and careless. Such as he was, his mother loved him with normal affection. She saw his weakness and tried to correct it. But she enjoyed his society, retained his confidence, and could be as merry with him as a summer's day, witness her inimitable account of his relating to her his comic parting from Ninon de l'Enclos. "He said the maddest things in the world and so did I. It was a scene worthy of Molière." Then, when he keeps bad company, behaves indiscreetly, and is generally reprehensible, she is aware of it at once and comments in no uncertain terms. "I wish you could see how little merit or beauty it takes to charm my son. His taste is beneath contempt."

But the daughter, the daughter, Madame de Grignan, she is a paragon, a miracle of nature, above admiration, and without defect. The bulk of Madame de Sévigné's correspondence is written to her, and what is much worse, it is written about her, page after page of advice, of anxiety, of adoration, until even dear lovers of the mother, like Fitzgerald, feel that, in her own vivid phrase, they have had "an indigestion of Grignans."

MADAME DE SÉVIGNÉ

But this feeling of boredom vanishes as soon as you see that you are confronted with a psychological problem. For Madame de Sévigné's attitude, her language, are not that of a normal, not even of a passionately affectionate, mother. Her feeling in this case is an obsession, a real mania, like a girl's or a grown woman's genuine love affair. She cannot be happy one moment away from the object of her devotion. She thinks of her daily, nightly, dreams of her, in everything is anxious to please her or sick to think she has not pleased her. She seeks solitude because there she can dream more freely of this beloved daughter of hers. And the chief charm of society is that some one may inquire about Madame de Grignan's health and venture a compliment which the eager listener can set down and pass on. Like a lover of twenty, she suggests that she and her beloved are looking at the moon at the same time. "You alone," she writes, in the ardor of her passion, "can make the joy or the sorrow of my life. I know nothing but you, and beyond you everything is nothing to me." Over and over again she repeats that she wishes she loved God as she loves this bit of herself, this thing of mortal, but exquisite fragility. Now this is not quite the love of a common sane and normal mother, is it?

And the daughter, did she deserve it? Some think not. She was beautiful. And she was a scholar, a pupil of Descartes, a reader of philosophies and critic of literature, who looked down a little on her mother's naïve and extremely personal judgments. She was a wit, also, — wrote what she thought fine letters. They seem to us a little stilted, as the one she sent to Moulceau after her mother's death. And some say she was haughty, without her mother's broad sympathy, and even high-tempered and quarrelsome.

But all these flaws were nothing to the mother lover. It is, indeed, pretty to observe how, being the keenest sighted of women, she occasionally sees things that she will not see. Thus, she writes of her daughter's boasted style, "It is perfect. All you have to do is to keep it as it is and not try to improve it." Or of her attitude towards herself. "Somebody said the other day that, with all the tender affection you have for me, you don't get as much out of my society as you might, that you do not appreciate what I am worth, even as regards you."

For the most part, however, it is a sweet, warm tempest of praise, an indigestion of praise, touchingly at variance with the chilly judgment of those who looked on. Madame de Grignan has not only the choicest of intellects, but the tenderest of hearts. She has a stoical, old Roman virtue which the vulgar may mistake for indifference; but underneath she is so surprisingly sensitive that every precaution is necessary to guard her too delicate nerves from intolerable shock. She thinks loftily, she speaks wittily, and her letters are the quintessence of everything finished and exquisite, so different from the hasty and careless scrawls of this scribbling mother, though, to be sure, good judges have found ours, also, not unworthy of commendation. And some, who do not believe that a love that takes us out of ourselves is the best worth having of all things in this loveless world, may think such a degree of self-deception puerile. It is a little unusual, at any rate.

Such a love, in a universe of cross accidents and unforeseen contingencies, is always shot through and through with misery. This woman, so poised and tempered in all that concerned herself and the common course of life, dwelt in a cloud of anxiety for what concerned the welfare of her precious daughter. It was worry, worry from morning till night. In far Provence, where the treasure and her husband and children lived, what disasters might not occur, while the sun was shining and wit sparkling in jovial Paris? With the lovely inconsistency of love, the mother declares at one moment that her passion is all joy and the delight of it far, far outweighs the care and trouble, at the next that life is only wretchedness for those who have a great devotion. "The mind should be at peace," she says; "but the heart debauches it perpetually. Mine is filled full with my daughter." She frets over great things and little, Madame de Grignan's children, Madame de Grignan's debts, Madame de Grignan's lawsuits, above all over Madame de Grignan's health. The daughter was, apparently, one of those persons who are never ill and never well. And the doting mother, at five hundred miles distance, is always suggesting drugs, draughts, plasters, poultices, doctors, doctor's devices, and devices of the devil.

Also, in the rare intervals when they were together she suggested to the same effect, and in consequence such sojourns were not happy. I know few things more tragic than this vast affection, longing, longing to be with its object, and when they did meet, thwarted, hampered, blighted by that fatal inadequacy of human contact which makes love's fine fruition a joy not of this transitory world. We have, of course, little record of things actually done or said while the lover and the beloved were together. But we have the piteous cry of the bereaved one when they had felt themselves compelled to part. "Was it a crime for me to be anxious about your health? I saw you perishing before my eyes, and I was not permitted to shed a tear. I was killing you, they said, I was murdering you. I must keep still, if I suffocated. I never knew a more ingenious and cruel torment." Or again, "In God's name, child, let us try another visit to reëstablish our reputation. We must be more reasonable, at least you must, and not give them occasion to say, 'You simply kill one another.'" With what a strangling clutch does she tear at her heart, in the effort to make those adjustments of human passion which can never be perfectly made by flesh and blood. "You speak like one who is even further from me than I thought, who has wholly forgotten me, who no longer understands the measure of my attachment, nor the tenderness of my heart, who knows no longer the devotion I have for her, nor that natural weakness and bent to tears which have been an object of mocking to your philosophic firmness."

But it makes no difference. In spite of presence, or absence, or indifference, the old wound keeps still and always fresh and bleeding. Still, still the longing heart cries out for what it needs, even if it can never obtain it.

MADAME DE SÉVIGNÉ

"How is it that my whole life turns on one sole thought and everything else appears to me to be nothing?" Only God can comfort her. "Everything must be given up for God, and I will do it, and will only wonder at His ways, who, when all things seem as if they should be well with us, opens great gulfs which swallow the whole good of life, a separation which wounds my heart every hour of the day and far more hours of the night than sense or reason would."

Thus, you see, this sweet and noble lady, whose robust strength it seems as if we might all envy, also carried her burden of spiritual grief. Assuredly she is the more charming for it. As she herself said: "In the midst of all my moralizing, I keep a good share of the frailty of humanity." Thank God, she did!

VII
Madame du Deffand

CHRONOLOGY

Marie de Vichy-Chamrond.
Born 1697.
Married Marquis du Deffand August 2, 1718.
Friendship with Mademoiselle de L'Espinasse
    1754–1764.
Met Horace Walpole 1765.
Died October 24, 1780.

Madame du Deffand

VII

MADAME DU DEFFAND

We know her intimately through her multitude of letters, but we know her only as a blind, infirm old woman, dependent on the kindness of others for amusement, if not for support, and ready to depart at any time from the well-worn and tedious spectacle of flavorless existence, if it had not been for her utter uncertainty as to the world that lay beyond.

She had been very young, however, very young and very gay, as traditions tell us. Born into the most dissipated period of French social life, the regency of the first half of the eighteenth century, she was conspicuous for her charm and wit as well as for the irregularity of her conduct. She is said to have been loved by the regent himself. In any case, she was most intimate with him and with his favorites, and turned that intimacy to advantage by securing a pension which was of solid value to her in later life. She fascinated others besides the wicked. The great preacher, Massillon, was summoned by her friends to convert her in early youth. He talked with her very freely, but would make no comment except that she was charming, and when asked to prescribe for her case would suggest nothing but a five-cent catechism.

She was married for convenience, but most inconveniently to her and her husband both. Either he was too fast for her, or too slow, at any rate he was too dull. She left him, and returned to him, and left him again, and was adrift in the wide world.

It is important to note that with Madame du Deffand, as with some other French women, extreme freedom of living is quite compatible not only with great refinement of taste, but with a singular delicacy and sensitiveness of moral perception. She has an occasional coarseness of speech belonging to her age, but few people have been more alive to fine shades of affection, of devotion, of spiritual tact.

Nevertheless, her early life must be remembered, if we would understand her later. She herself says, "Oh, I should not want to be young again on condition of being brought up as I was, living with the people I lived with, and having the sort of mind and character I have." Dissipation, even less innocent than hers, disorders life, strips it of illusion, takes away utterly and forever the charm of simple things.

With Madame du Deffand, at any rate, there was no illusion left, and in her gray old age the charm of simple things was gone and of complex also. If she could have detailed her chill philosophy to Rosalind, that child of dawn would have cried out even more than to the curious Jacques, "I had rather have a fool to make me merry than experience to make me sad." To this disillusioned lady the men and women of the age she lived in were either cynics or pedants, they were bold without force and licentious without merriment, they had little talent and a vast deal of presumption. But as far as her thought and her reading and her knowledge went, the men and women of other times were little better. Most were either fools or knaves and the few who were not were so painfully conscious of it that living with them was more of a burden than with the others. She has words more bitterly acrid than even La Rochefoucauld's to designate the folly and emptiness and wickedness of life. "I do not know why Diogenes went looking for a man: nothing could happen to him worse than finding one." And she sums it up in one terrible sentence. "For my part, I confess that I have but one fixed thought, one feeling, one misfortune, one regret, that ever I was born."

As a general thing, however, her complaint is less violent than this and what impresses her in life is not so much its actual evil and misery as its intolerable ennui. I must ask the reader's pardon for using the French word, which is, perhaps, by this time almost English. No equivalent exactly fits it. "Melancholy" suggests somewhat more of abstract reflection and "boredom" more of irritation with external circumstances. Both these are sometimes applicable, but one cannot get along without "ennui" in discussing Madame du Deffand.

This, then, is the deadly burden that life inflicts upon her. The great hours run by, immense, interminable, with nothing to fill them, nothing that inspires her, nothing that amuses her, nothing that distracts her even. The weary waste of time to come can be judged only by the barren memory of time past and that holds out neither encouragement nor hope. To be sure, she readily recognizes that the root of the trouble may be within. A certain lady fails to please her, "but she shared this misfortune with many others, for everything seems insupportable to me. This may very well be because I am insupportable myself." Whatever the cause, the malady is always present and without cure. "I end because I am sad with no reason for sadness except that I exist."

It might be supposed that, drifting always in such a dead fog of ennui, she might bore her correspondents, much more her readers among posterity. She does often. She would very much oftener, if she were not after all a Frenchwoman of the wittiest age of French social life, with the sparkle of French vivacity at the end of her pen. Feeble as she was, world-weary as she was, perhaps even in close connection with these conditions, she had an indomitable nervous energy, which responded in the most surprising way to social or spiritual stimulus. Horace Walpole speaks with admirable justice of her "Herculean weakness." She found life dull. Yet out of the dulness she could weave the tissue of a correspondence with Voltaire in which the balance of brilliancy is not always on one side. Could we say more? She goes right to the fact in her letters, speaks vigorously, without tautology, or circumlocution. "I care nothing for perfection of style or even for finished politeness. I detest phrases and energy delights me." With what verve and petulance does she express the emotion of the moment, grave or gay. "Quick, quick, quick, let me tell you about the supper of yesterday which worried me so for fear I should be dull, or crabbed, or embarrassed. Nothing of the sort. I never remember in all my life being younger, or gayer, or merrier."

She had the sheer salt of French wit, too, could tell a story inimitably, or strike off a stinging epigram. It was she who created the well-known phrase in regard to St. Denis's long perambulation with his head off: "It is the first step that costs"; she who said — untranslatably — of the verses that showered on Voltaire's grave, that the great author had become "*la pâture des vers*"; she who remarked of one of her own friends that her wit was like a fine instrument always a-tuning and never played on. Above all, she could make inexhaustible mockery of her besetting evil. "Write disagreeably, if you like," she urges. "As the man said of the rack, it will help me to pass an hour or two, at any rate." And again, "I hear nothings, I speak nothings, I take interest in nothing, and from nothing to nothing I travel gently down the dull way which leads to becoming nothing."

Thus the roses strewn over the abyss make it only deeper and blacker and more horrible. Others may take pleasure in her vivacity, may laugh at her stories and applaud her wit. She takes no pleasure and finds the applause and laughter utterly hollow. Man delights her not nor woman either. And still those interminable hours drag along, unfilled and unfillable as the sieves of the daughters of Danäus.

To be sure, when all these glittering analyses of nothing were written, she was old, and blind, and sleepless, three things that are apt to dull the quickest spirits. Before she was far past middle life her eyesight failed her and she became the frail, exquisite, touching figure that we see in her best-known portrait, sitting in a great straw-canopied chair, her *tonneau*, she called it, with fine, earnest, sensitive features, stretching out her hands in the groping gesture pathetically characteristic of her affliction. And loss of sight to eyes so keen must leave an appalling emptiness.

Also she was tormented by insomnia, to long, blind, empty days added solitary nights, when the tossing of weary limbs doubles the tossing of weary spirits. "One goes over and over in one's mind everything that worries and distresses one; I have a gnawing worm which sleeps no more than I do; I reproach myself alone with all my troubles and it seems clear that I have brought them all upon myself." At two A.M. such things do have a most intolerable clarity.

With afflictions like these, at seventy years old, it is perhaps not wonderful that a lone woman should feel she had had enough of life. Unfortunately Madame du Deffand's weariness began when she was young and could see — too well. According to Mademoiselle Aïssé, after she and her husband had parted, she asked him to come back to her, desiring to reëstablish her position in the world. For six weeks things hobbled along. Then she became bored till she could endure it no further, and she made her state of mind so evident, not by ill-temper, but by all signs of depression, that the husband departed, this time for good and all. But who can depict her experiences better than herself? "I remember thinking in my youth that no one was happy but madmen, drunkards, and lovers." And elsewhere she flings the facts at us like a glass of cold water in the face. "I was born melancholy. My gayety comes only by fits and they are growing rare enough."

Those things which distract and divert most men and women, those great passions and little pleasures which to some of us seem to fill every cranny of life with business and delight, to her meant simply nothing. If we review them in their larger categories, we shall see her lay her cold, light finger on them and shrivel them up. It is not deliberate on her part. She would be glad to enjoy as others do. But she has not the power. "It is not my purpose to refuse happiness from anything. I leave open every door that seems to lead to pleasure; and if I could, I would bar those that let in sorrow and regret. But destiny or fortune has bereft me of the keys that open and close the mansion of my soul."

Nature, the calmest, the most soothing of spiritual consolations? She has no place for it. As a scientific, intellectual pursuit, she blasts it with her savage, untranslatable epigram on Buffon: "*Il ne s'occupe que des bêtes; il faut l'être un peu soi-même pour se dévouer à une telle occupation.*" As for the emotional, imaginative aspects of the natural world, she grudgingly confesses that she might enjoy them, if circumstances were favorable: "I am not insensible to natural and rural beauties, but one's soul must be in a very gentle and peaceful mood to get much pleasure from them." Her friend, Horace Walpole, can hardly be regarded as an ardent nature lover, he who wrote of general birdsong, "It is very disagreeable that the nightingales should sing but half a dozen songs, and the other beasts squall for two months together." Yet to Madame du Deffand it seemed that even Walpole's delight in country life was quite incomprehensible. "I cannot form any idea of the pleasures you taste in solitude and of the charm you find in inanimate objects."

But the more human interests did not please her any better. Thought, learning, the long effort to understand the secret of life and the springs of human action? Will this dissipate ennui? Not hers. It only deadens it.

Politics? The movement of the world, wars, battles and sieges, deaths of illustrious princes and of unknown thousands? They move not her. High and mighty potencies seem to her perfectly trivial. "Let me whisper in your ear that I make precious little account of kings; their protestations, their retractations, their recriminations, their contradictions, I find them of no more moment than the mixing of a breakfast for my cat." But if you think that at the other extreme she had any more sympathy with the people, just then at the point of striving so mightily, you are altogether mistaken. "From the Agrarian Law down to your monument, your lanterns, and your black flag, the people, with its joy, its anger, its applause, and its curses, is thoroughly odious to me."

Then there is art, beauty of human creation, to some a resource so great that it overcomes not only tedium but even misery and acute suffering. To this lady with the dead heart beauty makes no appeal whatever. Her blindness of course cut her off from beauty of the eye to

which she seldom if ever refers. But the ears of the
blind are supposed to be doubly keen and indeed hers
were so. Yet to the nerves behind the ears music was
mainly a vexation. In one instance she does, indeed,
find the harp delightful. This was her idea of delight:
"The thought that one gets hold of nothing, that
everything slips away and fails us, that one is alone in
the universe and fears to go out of it: this is what occupied me during the music." Do you wonder that she
elsewhere writes, "To me music is a noise more impor-
tunate than agreeable."

With literature the case is little better. Madame du
Deffand knew well most of the French writers of her
day and had little esteem for them or their works. Of
earlier authors she thought more, but not much. La
Fontaine occasionally made her smile. Corneille's he-
roics enraptured her — for a moment. A minor comedy
gives her extreme pleasure, in fact she weeps during the
whole third act, and "they were not tears of bitter anguish, but tears of tender emotion." Her usual state
of mind is, however, better expressed in another passage: "Everything I read bores me; history, because I
am totally incurious; essays, because they are half
platitude and half affected originality; novels, because
the love-making seems sentimental and the study of
passion makes me unhappy."

For a soul thus blasted by a dry wind from the barren places of this world it would seem as if the thought
of another might offer irresistible attraction. It did,
and Madame du Deffand is fascinating on the subject.
She would like, oh, she would like to practice religion with

fervor. She invites a confessor to dine, talks with him, and is quite encouraged. Why should not grace work a miracle for her as well as for others? She reads Saint François de Sales and finds a tender and winning spirit under his "mystical nonsense." She regrets that he is dead. "He would have bored me considerably, but I should have loved him." And in her long hours of insomnia she reflects upon the delightful possibility of believing and builds castles in Spain, or in heaven. "I should read sermons instead of novels, the Bible instead of fables, the Lives of the Saints instead of history, and I should be less bored, or no more, than with what I read now . . . at least I should have an object to which I could offer all my sorrows and make the sacrifice of all my desires."

But it is utterly futile, babble of children, dreams of white nuns bereft of all converse with the heart of man. She was the pupil of Voltaire, the mistress of the Regent, the friend of D'Alembert and Helvétius. To be the friend of these celebrities and of God also would have been too much. Therefore she believed in nothing whatever. Faith, she says, is a devout belief in what one does not understand. We must leave it to those who have it. I have it not. And what belief could overcome the colossal wretchedness of having been born? "Everything that exists is wretched, an angel, an oyster, perhaps even a grain of sand; nothingness, nothingness, what better can we have to pray for?" She did not originate, but she would gladly have accepted the bitter definition of life as "a nightmare between two nothings."

Thus, you see, she missed, as so many do, the one great privilege of universal scepticism: universal hope. There are thousands who, like her, proclaim that they have no belief in anything, yet, like her, appear to have a most fervent belief in the devil and all his works.

It was natural that one isolated by blindness and unable to get pleasure from the resources of her own soul should turn to society, should try to draw life from constant contact with others who had more of it than she. In none was this restless desire ever more intense than in Madame du Deffand. She seeks people always, goes among them when she can, uses every effort to make them come to her. Her chief dread of poverty is that she may lose the means of attracting company. Even dull company seems to her more tolerable than her own thoughts. And as I have already pointed out, when she got among people, they enjoyed and admired her. She was quick, vivacious, brilliant, gave no sign of being bored, if she was so. Some of her words even make one suspect that she exaggerated her troubles and found more in life to please her than she would willingly confess. Hear what she says of a long projected and finally realized visit. "I have been here five weeks and I can say, with entire truth, that I have not been bored one single minute, have not had the smallest mishap or annoyance." Surely the most contented of us can seldom say as much.

But the general tone of her social experience is much better manifested in one long passage, as remarkable for style as for self-revelation. "Men and women alike seemed to me machines on springs, which went, came, spoke, laughed, without thinking, without reflecting, without feeling. Everybody played a part from habit merely. One woman shook with laughter, another sneered at everything, another gabbled about everything. The men's performance was no better. And I myself was swallowed up in the blackest of black thoughts. I reflected that I had passed my life in illusions; that I had dug for myself all the pits I had fallen into; that all my judgments had been false and rash, always too hasty; that I had never known any one perfectly; that I had never been known by any one either, and perhaps I did not know myself. One seeks everywhere for something to lean on. One is charmed with the hope of having found it: it turns out to be a dream which harsh facts scatter with a rude awakening."

By this time it must be very clear that the lady's worst tormentor was herself. If she could have followed the wholesome advice of her exquisite friend, Madame de Choiseul, she would have seen life differently. "Eat little at night, open your windows, drive out often, and look for the good in things and people. . . . You will no longer be sad, or bored, or ill." It was quite in vain. In such maladies the patient must minister to himself, and this poor patient not only submitted to the black ennui of to-day but doubled it, in fact gave it its chief significance, by dreading the longer, blacker hours of many to-morrows.

So you set her down as a cold, barren, dead old woman, and think you have heard enough of her. But there is more and of singular interest. She had noble and beautiful and winning qualities. For one thing, she was frank, straightforward, and sincere. Indeed, it was the excess of these fine traits that caused her troubles. She would have no illusion, no deception, no sham, nothing but the truth. It was the exaggerated fear of accepting pleasant falsehoods which led her to believe that necessarily everything pleasant must be a falsehood. But her honesty draws you to her, even while her misery repels.

Then, curiously enough, though the case is not unprecedented, her very pessimism and failure to find any good in the world resulted from an inherent idealism, from too high expectations of men and things. Her imagination was so keen that it discounted every pleasure before it came, with resultant disappointment. Her natural instinct was to trust, often unwisely. Then, when she was deceived, she mistrusted and suspected — unwisely also. Primarily she was a dreamer, a hoper, as she herself phrases it in her vivid language, "a listen-if-it rains, a visionary, who watches the clouds and sees lovely things there that fade even as one beholds them." And vast dreams dispelled left a darker and a sadder emptiness.

So with people. She demanded perfection, and would take nothing less. Men and women thus tempered go starved and discontented in this far from perfect world. "I pass in review everybody I know and everybody I have known; I do not see one of them without a fault, and I find myself worse than any of them." But, good heavens, what son or daughter of Adam can endure such a test as that? Yet some are extreme good company, nevertheless.

In other words, her bitter judgments were founded on an over-exacting standard and did not exclude pity or tenderness. Though too impatient to be of great help to others and too critical to be tolerant towards them, she was capable of keen and passionate sympathy, and she held kindness to be a great and most estimable virtue. With the candor which is one of her chief charms she confesses, "I renew every day the resolution to be kind and loving myself. How much progress I make I do not know."

And following this clue, if we probe still deeper, we come across a curious fact in Madame du Deffand's temperament, which seems to explain many things. Under all her misery, all her discontent, all her boredom, she was aching for love. Perhaps she was incapable of it. Perhaps her keen vision, and her deep mistrust, and her lofty demands on human nature made it impossible for her to give or to receive the passionate affection which might have filled her life. But after careful study it is impossible to resist the conclusion that she more than most women felt the deep need of all women, that the right home, and the right husband, and the right children might have given her the satisfaction she could not get from books, or thought, or art, or nature.

She herself recognized this, with lucidity as well as pathos. She repeats often that she loves nothing, less often that some inborn flaw, some unconquerable twist or imperfection, makes her incapable of loving anything. But far more often still does she cry out for love and tenderness. "Friendship is almost a mania with me; I was born for nothing else." "I love nothing and that is the true cause of my ennui." When she was dying, she saw her secretary, Wiart, who had long served her, in tears. "You love me, then?" she murmured, and so her last words expressed at once the doubt and the longing of her life.

Of her earlier attempts to satisfy this natural instinct three, at least, are well known to us and none was perfectly successful. For years she lived in the most intimate relations with Hénault, a man of the highest position and character; but he was not of a nature to feel ardor or inspire it. Their mutual attitude was one of respectful esteem, largely tempered with keen-sighted criticism. Again, Madame du Deffand took into her protection a young orphan relative, Mademoiselle de L'Espinasse, hoping to find a comfort for her age. But the older lady was exacting, the younger restless, and they quarreled and parted by the fault of both — or of neither. Finally, there was Madame de Choiseul, with whom it was not easy to quarrel. Madame du Deffand adored her, called her "grandmamma," though she was many years the younger, declared over and over again that her love was all she wanted, all her hope and comfort in life. Yet in one of her moments of desperate petulance she could write of even Madame de Choiseul: "She shows a good deal of friendship; and as she has none for me and I have none for her, it is perfectly natural that we should exchange the tenderest expressions in the world." Truly, a strange, subtle, and difficult temper, and one ill-fitted to separate the evil from the good in the tangled yarn of human life.

Then, after all these attempts at love and failures, came a most singular adventure. Madame du Deffand, at seventy, fell in love with a man of fifty. This world-worn, life-wearied, pale, frail, dusty heart was suddenly set beating by another as cold, as disillusioned, if not as bored as hers, that of Horace Walpole, a bachelor, a dilettante, and an Englishman. And this old woman's love was no mere fancy, no indifferent whim, lightly caught and blown off like a feather. It was a real, intense, absorbing, overwhelming passion, like that of a girl of twenty or a woman of forty. "Everybody loves after his own manner; I have only one way of loving, infinitely, or not at all." "The thought of you enters into everything I think and everything I do." This is the tone, not for an hour, or a day, but over and over and over, for eleven years. Let us note some of the special phases of such an unusual experience.

To begin with, how about Walpole himself? He was not infatuated. He never could have been, and certainly not at fifty, for an aged French-woman. He kept a cool head and saw with perfect clearness the foibles of his ardent correspondent. At the same time, his bearing in a rather difficult situation is on the whole loyal and manly. He defended his aged friend against criticism and mockery and it is from him that we get the finest appreciation of her good qualities, her noble sincerity, her unconquerable vivacity, her social charm.

But if he sees her as we see her, assuredly she does not see him as we see him, or never, never admits that she does. Without accepting all of Macaulay's severe judgment, it is difficult to place Walpole on a very heroic plane. He was kindly, he was gentle, he was generous where it cost him little, he was mildly loyal to his friends. But he was vain, superficial, snobbish while pretending to democracy, incapable of great devotion and of self-forgetfulness. The Walpole that Madame du Deffand loved was, however, far different from this. He had the virtues of French and English combined and the vices of no race. As an author, he is in the same class with Voltaire, his letters are like Voltaire's for style, and far above for matter. "For style they have had no model and cannot be imitated. They are the sublime of abundance and of naturalness." If you know Walpole, what do you think of that? And his character is as sublime as his letters. He is perhaps a little godlike for perfect friendship, or is she wrong about this? But in the early stages of her passion she proclaims the lover's idea from which she never swerves. "If others saw as clearly as I do, you would be placed first, not only in England, but in the universe; this is not flattery; wit, talent, and the perfection of kindness have never been united as they are in you." What a marvellous light is thrown on the woman's character, as we have studied it, by such a sentence as that!

So she plays, in letter after letter, on the whole compass of the tenderest, most self-abandoning affection. With him in London and herself in Paris, and several days of delaying post between them, she writes incessantly, begging for good news, bad news, any news. His plans, she must know every detail of his plans, what he does, where he goes, whom he sees. His health.

Let but the gout touch him and she is in misery. She showers remedies, like a quack doctor, or an aged nurse. Her distress is everywhere made plain to us by the vivid touches of her quick imagination. "I am like a child hanging out of a window by a cord and every instant on the brink of falling."

The best remedy for the anxiety of absence would certainly be presence and she seems to live only in the passionate hope of those rare and hurried visits which brought her beloved to her. Yet even so, she is most characteristically afraid that when he does come he will be bored. He shall see only whom he wishes when he wishes, provided he gives long hours to seeing her. He comes, she is in Paradise, sits talking with him till two in the morning, and he gets a long letter from her before he rises the next day.

Then he is gone again and she is in pain again. The memory of past pleasure only makes the pang of separation keener. She is old, old, hardly a particle of life left in her, and she cannot hope to live to see him ever any more.

A passion like this, full as it is of tragedy and pathos, will at times tempt sarcasm. The sincerity and fine intelligence of Madame du Deffand make it impossible for a sympathetic reader even to smile at her. But Walpole was by nature abnormally sensitive to ridicule, as he himself confesses. To be praised as if he were a god and loved as if he were an opera tenor by an old lady of seventy, whom he knew to be living in closest intimacy with the most critical and mocking wits of the world, placed a man of his temper in an exceedingly difficult position. Beware of romance, he cautioned mildly. But she laughed at him. Romance! at her age! She had never been romantic, had all her life stripped the veil of sentimental illusion from the cold bones of reality. Romance! Her feelings were nothing but common, daylight friendship. In which she was quite wrong, for nothing about her was or could be common or of every day.

So felt Walpole. And he still shuddered at the thought of the vast guffaw of future generations. Destroy my letters, he insisted, and do, do moderate the tone of yours. And he cautioned, and he lectured, as a tutor might lecture a moonstruck girl.

She did not like it, she resented it. The notes she writes so thickly are of painful interest in their sore, hurt, pleading, protesting energy. "If I were as unreasonable as you, you would never hear another word from me. The letter I have just received is so offensive, so extravagant, that I should throw it in the fire unanswered." "Should throw," you notice, not "have thrown." "It is impossible to judge more falsely than you judge me. . . . You see yourself in everything I say about others and think I am finding fault with you, when I find fault with any one." "God is not more incomprehensible than you; but if he is not more just, it is hardly worth while believing in him."

Yet she kissed the hand that chastened her, she turned like a child to its tutor, for advice and comfort, with blind trust, blind confidence, blind hope. He is a true physician for the soul, she says, and one who needs no physician for his own. She only wishes that he might have had control of her from childhood. How different she would have been! "You would have formed my taste, my judgment, my discernment, you would have taught me to know the world, to mistrust it, to despise it, to enjoy it; you would not have bridled my imagination, or blighted my passions, or chilled my soul; but you would have been like a skilful dancing-master, who keeps the natural poise of health and vigor and adds to it finished grace."

So she loved for eleven years and died with this final illusion like the cross in her hands and the sacred wafer at her lips. You think she was pitiably infatuated. Perhaps she was. But it was an infatuation that not only furnished the clue to her whole life, but in a manner sanctified it.

It is a curious thing that the two greatest women letter writers of France, perhaps of the world, Madame de Sévigné and Madame du Deffand, should each have built the main fabric of their correspondence on an exaggerated, not to say abnormal, affection. It is far more curious that this affection should be with Madame de Sévigné the one flaw in a singularly well-balanced character and with Madame du Deffand the most marked symptom of health in a character otherwise erratic, distorted, and unsound.

VIII
Madame de Choiseul

CHRONOLOGY

Louise Honorine Crozat du Châtel.
Born 1734.
Married Duc de Choiseul 1750.
Choiseul's ministry 1758–1770.
Husband died 1785.
Died December 3, 1801.

Madame de Choiseul

VIII

MADAME DE CHOISEUL

A PORTRAIT of Madame de Choiseul seems the natural complement to the portrait of Madame du Deffand. The two were intimate friends, in spite of a considerable difference in age; their lives were intertwined in the closest fashion. At the same time, they present a marked contrast in temperament, character, and habits of thought. Madame du Deffand's estimate of her younger friend, whom she playfully called "grandmamma," will serve well to set the note for a portrayal of the latter: "If there is a perfect being in the world, 't is she. She has mastered all her passions. No one is at once so sensitive and so completely mistress of herself. Everything is genuine in her, nothing artificial, yet everything is under control."

Elsewhere Madame du Deffand points out that if Madame de Choiseul was perfect, she had everything to make her so, family, fortune, friends, and social position. "I know no one who has been so continuously and so completely fortunate as you." In a sense this was exact. Madame de Choiseul from birth filled a high position in the social life of the French mid-eighteenth century. She married early a man of the greatest distinction and charm, who came to occupy the most important political offices, and for a time she was perhaps the leading lady of France, next the queen —

and the king's mistress. But her life was not all roses, by any means. Her husband was charming to others as well as to her. She had no children. Politics brought her misery as well as fortune, since the duke lost his office and was sent in disgrace and banishment from court. Later he died and she was left alone to face the Revolution, which she did with the splendid patience and courage shown by so many women of her class. But this was long after Madame du Deffand had exchanged the ennui of earth for the felicity of heaven.

During the time she held a leading social position, Madame de Choiseul proved to be in every way fitted for it. She herself declares she has no preference for such a life, complains that her hours are filled not occupied, longs for solitude and quiet, and when they come, as a result of political failure, accepts them with a sigh of genuine relief.

But all agree that for the manifold uses of society she had a singular aptness and charm. She was married when she was fifteen, and at eighteen went as ambassadress to Rome, where she made herself beloved by every one. She was not perhaps regularly beautiful, but her little figure had a fairylike grace and lightness, and her simple, dainty speech and manners doubled the attraction of her figure. "A Venus in little," *Vénus en abrégé*, Voltaire calls her. Horace Walpole, who to be sure loved all the friends of Madame du Deffand, says of the duchess: "Oh, it is the gentlest, amiable, civil, little creature that ever came out of a fairy egg! So just in its phrases and thoughts, so attentive and good-natured!" Elsewhere he is even

more enthusiastic: "She has more sense and more virtues than almost any human being," and another brief
touch gives a climax quite unusual with the cynic of
Strawberry Hill: "The most perfect being I know of
either sex."

Nor was this grace and perfection of the tame order
which effaces itself and merely warms others till they
sparkle and flame. The lady had a fairy's vivacity as
well as a fairy's daintiness. It is true, social embarrass-
ment sometimes overcame her — most winningly. She
had, says Walpole further, "a hesitation and modesty,
the latter of which the court has not cured, and the
former of which is atoned for by the most interesting
sound of voice, and forgotten in the most elegant turn
and propriety of expression." She herself gives a
charming account of a social crisis in which she was
utterly at a loss what to do or say and could only
stammeringly repeat the words of others, "Yes, Madam, no, Madam, — I think, that is, I believe — oh,
yes, I am sure I agree with you entirely."

But she had wit of her own, spirit of her own, courage
of her own, and could find words in plenty when occasion really called for them. Madame du Deffand has
preserved many of her clever sayings, as the comment
on two gentlemen equally amiable, but different. "One
is charming for the manner that he has and the other
for the manner that he has not."

The lasting evidence for us, however, of Madame de
Choiseul's vivacity is her letters. They exist in no
such number as Madame du Deffand's or Madame de
Sévigné's, but they yield to neither in ease, in vari-

ety, in grace and swiftness of expression. These qualities are equally manifest in her long description of the busy day of a prime minister's wife, — the scores of petitioners, the hurry from one function to another, the tedious necessity of being something to everybody while nobody is anything to you,— and in little touches of the most pregnant and delicate simplicity. "What is there to say in the country when you are alone and it rains? We were alone and it was raining. This suggested talk of ourselves and, after all, what is there that we know so much about?" or again, "To love and to please is to be always young." She could and did write French as perfect as Voltaire's. But she did not hesitate a moment to twist grammar or syntax, when some unusual turn of thought required it. "I propose to speak my own tongue before that of my nation," she says, "and it is often the irregularity of our thought that causes the irregularity of our expressions."

But it was neither her beauty nor her wit that made the duchess so much admired and beloved. It was her sympathy and tenderness, her faculty of entering into the joys and sorrows of others and her pleasure in doing so, that drew all hearts to her. "She had the art of listening and of making others shine," says a memoir writer of her own day. This is a social quality by no means contemptible. But the quality of sympathetic comprehension served for much more than social purposes. "I cannot bear the idea of suffering, even for persons indifferent to me," she writes. This did not mean, however, that she fled suffering, but that she endeavored to alleviate it, by every means in her power.

MADAME DE CHOISEUL

Where the suffering was mental or imaginary, she soothed and diverted it by sound counsel and gentle rallying, if necessary. Where it was physical, she gave her time and thought and strength to substantial relief.

Her dependents, her servants, the poor in all the region round, adored her. She gave them money, she gave them food, she gave them the sunshine of her presence and her cheerfulness. A servant whose work had been about the house was offered a better position outside. He refused it. "But why," urged the duchess, "why? Your pay will be better, your hours shorter, your work lighter." "Yes, madam, but I shall not be near you." After the Revolution, when she had lost everything and was living in a garret, there came one day a knock at the door. She opened it to a rather prosperous-looking mechanic, and inquired what he wanted. "Madam, when I was a poor peasant, working on the roads, you asked me what I desired most in the world. I said, a cart and an ass to draw it. You gave them to me and I have made a comfortable fortune. Now it is all yours."

If she was thus kind to those who were nothing to her personally, it may well be supposed that she was devoted to her friends. She had many of them and never felt that she had enough. Like all persons of such ample affection, she had her disappointments, with resulting cynicism, and once wrote: "It is well to love even a dog when you have the opportunity, for fear you should find nothing else worth loving." But in general, though she was far from indiscriminate in her choice, she loved widely, and she repeats again and again that love is the only thing that makes life worth living, that love is life. When the bitter saying of Madame de Staël is reported to her, that she was always glad to make new acquaintances because she felt sure they could not be worse than those she had already, Madame de Choiseul rebels with the utmost indignation, declaring that she is not dissatisfied with any of her acquaintance and that she is enchanted with her friends. It seems, also, that her friendship was to a singular degree sympathetic and self-forgetful. So many of us see our friends' lives from the point of view of our own and enter into their interests chiefly so far as they are identical with ours. But this lady has one beautiful and perfect word on the subject: "I have always had the vanity of those I love, that is my fashion of loving."

One of her friendships we can study in minute detail and we find it to be without fault or flaw, that for Madame du Deffand. One friend was young, rich, beautiful, popular, driven in the rush and hurry of the great world. The other was old, feeble, blind, forlorn. Yet the friendship was as genuine and heartfelt on one side as on the other. Madame de Choiseul had the discernment to see Madame du Deffand's fine qualities, her clear head, her tender heart, her magnificent sincerity; but she cherished her, as love does cherish, not from a mathematical calculation of fine qualities, but simply because it does and must. I love you, she repeats, I love you. I think of you daily, hourly. Tell me everything, as I tell you everything. Let there be no secrets and no shadows between us.

MADAME DE CHOISEUL

Nor was it by any means an untested friendship. Madame du Deffand had nothing to do but think of trouble, she was critically sensitive, knew her own weaknesses, and could not believe that anybody loved her. Often she intimates her complaints, her dissatisfaction, her jealousy. Madame de Choiseul is sometimes forced to treat her like the child she calls her. There are moments when a frank, outspoken word is necessary. But it is spoken with careful tenderness. "You think I love you from complaisance and ask you to visit me from politeness. I don't. I love you because I love you. I will not say because you are lovable; for your fears, your doubts, your absurd hesitations annoy me too much for compliments. I don't care about doing you justice. I want to do justice to myself. I love you because you love me, because I have my own interests at heart, and because I am absolutely sure of you. . . . I want to see you, because I love you, right or wrong." And she did love her, in spite of all criticism and difficulty, with patient tenderness, thoughtful devotion, and infinite solicitude, till the very end.

Another friendship, of a somewhat different character, but of almost equal interest, is that for the Abbé Barthélemy, the clever, brilliant, sensitive scholar who was dependent upon the duchess's bounty during a great part of his life. Here again, in the Abbé's enthusiastic descriptions and comments, we see the thoughtful kindness, the unselfish devotion, the unobtrusive sympathy, which Madame de Choiseul lavished on those whom she had taken into her heart.

Sometimes this tenderness got her into difficulties. She added a child, apt and skilled in music, to her household, and made a pet of him. As he grew older, the boy fell in love with her, and she did not know what to do about it. Her pathetic account of her attempts to reason with him should be read in the original to be appreciated: "He could eat nothing, he could attend to nothing, and one day I found him seated at the clavichord, his heart overflowing in pitiful sighs. I called him, 'my sweet child,' to pet him and comfort him a little. Then his heart failed him and his tears flowed abundantly. Through a thousand sobs I could make out that he reproached me for calling him 'my sweet child,' when I did n't love him and would n't let him love me. . . . My courage broke too, I cried as much as he did, and to hide my tears I ran to find Monsieur de Choiseul and told him the whole story."

Some gossips attempted to see in this pretty incident a suggestion, or at any rate a parallel, to the adventures of the page, Cherubino, in Beaumarchais's "Marriage of Figaro," written at a later date. Such slander was utterly unfounded. It is not the least of Madame de Choiseul's charms that in an age when to have only one lover at a time was virtue and to have many was hardly vice, she is absolutely above the suspicion of having had any lovers at all. No doubt she knew that she was charming and liked to be admired. Madame du Deffand was perfectly right in reproaching Walpole for the singular lack of tact implied in his compliment to the duchess's virtue. "Why did you tell her that a man would never think of falling in love with her? No woman under forty likes to be praised in that fashion." But she herself declares that she was something of a prude and the testimony of many besides Walpole proves conclusively that she was not the opposite.

Moreover, she had the best of guarantees against waywardness of the affections, a profound, enduring, and self-forgetful love for her husband. Walpole cynically suggests that this love was too obtrusive to be sincere. In Walpole's world such obtrusiveness may not have been fashionable. "My grandmamma has the ridiculous foible of being in love," says Madame du Deffand. Some may not find it so ridiculous. At any rate, to the duchess her husband was the most important figure in the world and the obvious delight with which she welcomes political banishment because it means solitude and seclusion with him is as charming as it is pathetic.

Pathetic, because she did not get the same devotion in return. The duke loved her, respected her, admired her. His serious words about her are worthy of him and her both: "Her virtues, her attractions, her love for me and mine for her, have brought to our union a happiness far beyond the gifts of fortune." But, though a prime minister, the duke was not always serious, in fact too seldom. He was a brilliant, versatile, gay, and amorous Frenchman, and while he loved his wife, which was a merit, he loved many other ladies, which was less so. "He does not mean to go without anything," writes the duchess to Madame du Deffand, in a moment of unusual frankness. "He lets no pleas-

ure escape him. He is right in thinking that pleasure
is a legitimate end, but not every one is satisfied with
pleasures that come as easily as his. Some of us cannot get them for merely stooping to pick them up."

Yet, with all his weaknesses, it cannot be said that
the passionate lover had chosen a wholly unworthy
object, and even if she had, the breadth, the inten-
sity, the nobility of her passion would have gone far
to justify it. How tactful she is, with all her longing
for affection! She does not intrude her feelings at the
wrong place or time. She thinks more of giving than
of getting. How exquisitely tender are the gleams we
see, often through others, of the devotion which showed
itself in a hundred little forms of the desire to please.
"Your grandmamma is at the clavichord," writes
Barthélemy, with playful exaggeration, "and will
remain there till dinner time. She will go at it again at
seven and play till eleven. She has been doing this for
two months, with infinite pleasure. Her sole object is
to get so she can play to the duke without nervousness. To accomplish that result will take her about
fourteen years longer, and she will be perfectly satisfied if at fifty she can play two or three pieces without
a slip."

Her own words are even more significant. "I want to
grow young again, and pretty, if I could. At any rate,
I should like to make your grandpapa think I am both
one and the other, and as he has little here to compare me with, I may be able to deceive him." Again,
in as charming a bit of self-revelation as it would be
easy to find, she writes to Madame du Deffand, with a

lover's passionate urgency: "Tell me, dear grandchild, did your grandpapa come back again Wednesday, after he had put me into the carriage? Did he speak of me? What did he say and how did he say it? I can't help thinking that he grows a little less ashamed of me, and it is a great point gained when we no longer mortify those whom we would have love us. — You must admit that your grandpapa is the best of men; but that is not all, I assure you he is the greatest man the age has produced."

If he was not, at least she did her best to make him so. While he was minister, she pulled every wire a loving woman can pull honestly, even stooping to court and caress Madame de Pompadour, the mistress of the king. When he was disgraced, she cherished his friends and fought his enemies, minimized his faults and blazoned his virtues, believed in him so intensely that she made others believe who were much more ready to doubt. After his death, she sold her possessions and lived in poverty to pay his debts and clear his memory. When she was urged to flee during the Revolution, she said she could not, or those debts would never be paid, and when she was imprisoned and in danger of the guillotine, her plea for release was still that she had a task to do on earth that was not done. She was set free and continued her efforts till her death.

It will be asked if this charming personage had no faults. Of course she had. She realized them herself, and so did others. It was even maintained that her very faultlessness was an imperfection and that she overcame nature so completely as to be not quite human enough. The Abbé Barthélemy himself, loyal and devoted as he was, and protesting that he is a monster of ingratitude, whispers gently to Madame du Deffand that his patroness had serious defects, to be sure chiefly injurious to herself, which resulted from her very excess of virtue, sympathy, and self-control. Elsewhere he murmurs that she is so busy with everybody it is sometimes hard to realize that she cares for anybody, and again that she thinks so much of friends who are absent that those who are present get very little attention.

Madame du Deffand, who was lonely, sensitive, and jealous, is much more free in her criticism. Persons overflowing with sympathy and kindness, like Madame de Choiseul, are always exposed to the charge of insincerity and the older friend expresses this, in the early days of their acquaintance, with the utmost bitterness. "She makes a great show of friendship. And as she has none for me and I have none for her, it is perfectly natural that we should say the tenderest things possible to one another."

The passage of years wholly corrected this misapprehension. The blind, forlorn, love-thirsty dreamer came to know that there was no love in the world more loyal, more tender, more self-forgetful than that of this wonderful lady who might have had princes at her feet. Yet the solitary heart is not contented, can never be contented. Soothing, petting, rallying may calm it for the moment. It will never be still. "You cannot let go in your letters. You always say just what you want to say." She writes grumblingly to Walpole of the duchess: "She wants to be perfect. That is her defect." And again, "It is vexatious that she is an angel. I had rather she were a woman." The sum total of the complaint recurs again and again in a phrase which Madame de Choiseul had most unfortunately invented herself. "You know you love me, but you do not feel it."

Yet, after all, the lady was not so fatally angelic as to lose every appeal to frail humanity. It stung her to be dependent. It stung her to ask a favor of an enemy. It stung her to have any one ask a favor for her. With what wholesome vigor does she lash Madame du Deffand, who had innocently spoken a kind word for her friend to the wife of her friend's chief political antagonist. "This is something I will not allow. This is something you absolutely must make right, and in the presence of the very persons who were witnesses to a piece of cajolery so unfitting under existing circumstances and so utterly foreign to my character." And she adds, "the Abbé, who is all for gentle methods, will try to smooth this over. But, for my part, though I am sorry to hurt you, I don't retract a word, because I have said what I feel."

Also, she was capable of good honest hatred, when she thought there was occasion for it, and right in the family too. Her husband had a sister, Madame de Grammont, a big haughty Juno, if the duchess was a little Venus, and between the two there was no friendship. The duke hearkened to the sister much more than the wife liked. In short, they were jealous of each other and though they finally patched up an armed truce which age developed into a reconciliation, they never regarded each other with much cordiality. How vividly human is Madame de Choiseul's account of her conduct when the duke had an attack of illness. "Though I hate Madame de Grammont, I sent her word, because I should wish her to do the same to me. What happened? She hever thanked me, she never even answered me, but wrote to the duke to complain that he had not written and thus got me into trouble."

So, you see, she knew the bitter emotions of life as well as the sweet, and was by no means exempt from any aspect of human frailty. Yet, although her soul was wide-open to emotions of all sorts, and though she herself passionately repeated that feeling was the only good of existence, was the whole of existence, she had, beside her emotions, an intellectual life singularly subtle, plastic, and varied, and full of interest to the curious student. She was apt to condemn reason as misleading, deceptive, and of little worth, but in demonstrating the point she indulged herself in reasoning of a highly elaborate and ingenious order. In fact, she was a child of the eighteenth century, and could not wholly escape its abstract tendencies. Speaking of her own letters, when a friend wanted to collect them for publication, she said, "to me they seem to be the writing of a *raisonneuse.*"

She came naturally by this argumentative tendency, for it was said of her father that he was too inclined to dissect his ideas and had a leaning toward metaphysics which he communicated to his wife, so that the daughter's cradle may have been rocked by tempests of theoretical discussion. She herself declares that she was not educated at all and thanks heaven for it. For, she says, at least she was not taught the errors of others. "If I have learned anything, I owe it neither to precepts nor to books, but to a few opportune misfortunes. Perhaps the school of misfortunes is the very best." She had, however, picked up a rather broad learning through keen attention and a love of books. She speaks of Pliny, Horace, Cicero, and other Latin authors, as if she knew them by heart. She reads the Memoirs of Sully with delight, though chiefly why? Because Sully's situation reminds her of Monsieur de Choiseul's. She deplores Madame du Deffand's indifference to reading: "Books help us to endure ignorance and life itself: Life, because the knowledge of past wretchedness helps us to endure the present; ignorance, because history tells us nothing but what we already know." Here you see the touch of the *raisonneuse*, to use her own phrase, the curious analyst, the minute dissector of her own motives and those of others. Madame du Deffand quotes a German admirer as saying of the duchess: "She is reason masquerading as an angel and having the power to persuade with charm."

It is most fruitful to follow the gleaming thread of Madame de Choiseul's analysis through the different concerns and aspects of human life.

Of art she apparently knew nothing whatever. Though herself a figure just stepped out of a canvas of Watteau, she never mentions him, nor any other artist, greater or lesser. We do not see that plastic

beauty existed for her at all. Of her music we know only
that she practised day and night to please her husband.
Nature she never mentions in any aspect. All that
she has to say of her long years in the country is that
solitude is restful.

On the other hand, she shows much of herself and
of her own mind in what she says of literature. As we
have seen, she was a good deal of a reader, would have
read much more, or fancied she would, if she had not
had a thousand other things to do. And her judgment
of books and authors is as keen and penetrating as it
is independent. It shows further the strong, sound,
moral bent of her disposition. She pierces Rousseau's
extravagant theorizing about nature with swift thrusts
of practical sense, summing up her verdict in a touch
of common truth expressed inimitably: "Let us beware
of metaphysics applied to simple things." And Rousseau himself she defined with bitter accuracy: "He has
always seemed to me to be a charlatan of virtue." Voltaire she judged with a singular breadth and justice
of perception, appreciating to the full his greatness and
his pettiness. "He tells us he is faithful to his enthu-
siasms; he should have said, to his weaknesses. He has
always been cowardly where there was no danger, in-
solent where there was no motive, and mean where
there was no object in being so. All which does not pre-
vent his being the most brilliant mind of the century.
We should admire his talent, study his works, profit by
his philosophy, and be broadened by his teaching. We
should adore him and despise him, as is indeed the case
with a good many objects of worship."

MADAME DE CHOISEUL

This passage alone would show that we are dealing with a vigorous and independent mind. The impression is by no means diminished when we read the duchess's other outpourings on abstract subjects. Some indeed think that she overdoes the matter, that she has caught the pernicious eighteenth-century habit of moral declamation, in short, that she violated her own excellent precept about applying metaphysics to simple things. But her sight was so clear, her sympathy so tender, and her heart so sound that I do not think any one can seriously accuse her of being a rhetorician.

It is, however, very curious to compare her in this respect with Madame du Deffand, who takes no interest whatever in general questions, and is disposed to leave politics to princes, religion to priests, and the progress of mankind to those who can still believe in it. Not so Madame de Choiseul. She thinks passionately on the great problems of life and history and follows with keen interest the thinking of others. When Voltaire sets himself up as the apologist of Catherine II of Russia, the duchess's sense of right is outraged and in a strange long letter to Madame du Deffand she analyzes Catherine's career and with it the whole theory of political and social morals. When Rousseau is under discussion, she analyzes carefully the tissue and fabric of organized community life. When forms of government attract her pen, she analyzes monarchy and democracy and expresses a sympathy with the latter surprisingly significant for her age and class. When her analyzing appetite can find no other bone to gnaw on, she analyzes her own happiness, with the subtlety of La

Bruyère. Perhaps the following is a little too much an application of metaphysics to simple things: "Gayety, even when it is habitual, seems to me only an accident. Happiness is the fruit of reason, a tranquil condition, and an enduring one, which knows neither transport nor ecstasy. Perhaps it is a slumber of the soul, death, nothingness. As to that I cannot say, but by these words I mean nothing sad, though people commonly think of them as lugubrious."

In all these elaborate analyses it is noticeable that there is no trace whatsoever of religion. Madame de Choiseul was as completely sceptical as Madame du Deffand. In all their correspondence God is hardly mentioned, even in the light, intimate way so common with the French. Madame de Choiseul declares her uncertainty with perfect frankness. "My scepticism has grown so great that it falls over backward and from doubting everything I have become ready to believe everything. For instance, I believe just as much in Blue Beard, the Thousand and One Nights, genii, fairies, sorcerers, and will-o'-the-wisps, as in — what shall I say? — anything you please." Nor is her faith in human nature in the abstract any more stable, as soon as she subjects it to the cold ray of her analyzing intellect. "Let us say once for all that there are few people whom one can count on, a melancholy truth that chills the heart and withers the confidence of youth. We grow old as soon as we cease to love and trust." While her summing up of the acme of possible good wishes is, to say the least, not of a very spiritual tenor. "Good-by, dear child, I wish you good sleep and a good digestion. I don't know anything better to desire for those I love."

What is deeply important and significant for the study of Madame de Choiseul in this lack of positive belief is that on a substructure apparently so frail there could be built up a character so rounded, so pure, so delicate, so eminently self-forgetful and devoted. And it is to be observed that her perfection was not all the result of a happy, contented, optimistic temperament. She was not born entirely a saint, nor quite ignorant of the perversities of frail humanity. She herself says: "With a warm heart which longed for affection and a quick imagination which must be ever at work, I was more disposed to unhappiness and ennui than people usually are. Yet I am happy and ennui gets no hold on me." In many other passages she makes it evident that she had her troubles, many of them. Physically, she was delicate and sensitive, always ailing, and it is a charming bit of human nature that with all her splendid self-control she could not refrain from eating things that disagreed with her, so that Barthélemy complains that she had the courage of a lion in great matters and was a coward in little. Also, the seeds of spiritual complaints were manifestly latent in her and she had her dark hours when sadness and anxiety and regret threatened to assert themselves with irresistible vigor. She speaks somewhere, as the years roll on, of "the terror which seizes me and the disgust which overpowers me when I see the work of destruction advancing and that resistance is no longer equal to attack."

But to all these subtle dangers she opposed a superb strength of will, a splendid courage, and above all the instinctive, unconquerable, eternal energy of love. While she was doing something for others she was happy and for others there was always something to be done. It is a most satisfying and tranquilizing thing to see a creature so dainty, so exquisite, so finely tempered with all the delicate responsiveness we now-a-days call nerves, at the same time steeled and toughened by that substantial necessity, common sense. She knew all the good of life and all the evil. Beauty, rank, wealth, love, honor, exile, ruin, and disaster were all hers. And through them all she remained the same simple, gentle, loyal, heroic figure, admirable if a woman ever was, and memorable if the highest charm backed by the strongest character are indeed worth remembering.

IX
Eugénie de Guérin

CHRONOLOGY

Eugénie de Guérin.
Born in Languedoc, 1805.
Visited Paris 1838.
Brother died 1839.
Visited Paris 1841.
Died May, 1848.

IX

EUGÉNIE DE GUÉRIN

SHE lived a solitary, an almost eremitical life, utterly secluded from the contact, and almost from the knowledge, of the great world. No isolation in America to-day could be quite so complete as that of a lady in a French provincial town a hundred years ago: the same quiet waysides, the same faces at the same corners the same seasons in their eternal change, the bell of centuries tolling a monotonous succession of births, marriages, and deaths. All the varied doings of mankind in hasty cities, kings crowned and uncrowned, new thoughts, new fashions, new vices, new beauty, echoed in that tranquil dwelling like the far passage of some martial pageant stirring a dream. "Two visits, two letters written, one received, fill a day," she says; "fill a day full for us."

She did not complain of the solitude, she loved it. She was born in it, grew up in it, and wished to die in it. Every tree, every flower was a friend to her. Old sunlit walls caressed her with a touch like love's. "I could take a vow to remain here forever," she says. "No place could be to me so much my home." The habit of loneliness grows on her, as all our habits do, until one day, returning to a house quite empty, she exclaims, "You cannot think how gaily I took possession of this abandoned dwelling. Here I am alone, absolutely alone, in a place which of itself breeds calm reflection. I hear the passers pass, and do not even turn my head."

In a life so unbroken little movements made a great stir. Twice she sojourned for a few weeks in Paris and she made a brief visit to a watering place in the Pyrenees. On all these occasions she was quick and wide-eyed to catch what went on about her. She responded to great scenes and notable monuments and was not incurious as to the ways of men and women. But she felt no eagerness to change her own habits and returned with undisturbed delight to the places she had always loved. "Repose is what delights me; not inaction, but the poised quiet of a heart that is content."

Do not imagine that her solitude meant always quiet, however. Such outward peace perhaps fosters inward turbulence, at any rate leaves room for it. Hearts unvexed by the world's rash hurry have tempests and revolutions and tumults all their own. How many strange soul-combats go on in quiet tenements! How many fierce struggles pass unperceived and unrecorded, perhaps not worth recording, yet of immense significance to those who conquer or succumb! "All my days are alike, so far as the outer world goes," writes Mademoiselle de Guérin; "but with the soul's life it is different, nothing could be more varied, more flexible, more subject to perpetual change."

Two main, essential objects of all her inner life and thought kept her in this unceasing agitation. One was her brother Maurice. She had another brother and a sister whom she loved and cherished. To her father she

was a sympathetic companion and a faithful attendant. But Maurice was confessedly more to her than
any one else. He was younger than she. She had supplied for him the place of the mother who died early.
She tended him, watched over him, guided him, and
when he went out into the great world thought of him
and prayed for him perpetually.

He was one who well deserved such affection. Sensitive, delicate in health and in feeling, imaginative,
finely touched to all the fine issues of genius, his brief
life was torn and tortured by alternate aspiration and
doubt, by vast dreams of what he might achieve and
miserable distrust of his ability to achieve anything.
He died young and left behind him a journal recording
these struggles with pathetic fidelity and one short
prose poem, which has wide harmonies of classic dignity and echoing grandeur not surpassed by the "Hype-
rion" of Keats. Who that knows that music can ever
forget it? "*O Mélampe! les dieux errants ont posé leur
lyres sur les pierres; mais aucun — aucun ne l'y a oubliée.*"

The sister also kept a journal. But while Maurice's
was addressed to himself or to curious posterity, hers
was addressed only to him; even after death had
snatched him from her, only to him. All her inmost
thoughts go there, all her hopes, all her sorrows, and
to pour them out to him is the great preoccupation of
her life. She can say to him things she cannot say to
others. He will understand. He has always understood.
With great and with little events it is the same. A sun-
set walk in the fields and the death of a dear friend —
each alike must be discussed with Maurice. All the

emotion each brings with it must be confided to him. Anxiety for his health, for his future, for his happiness, is constantly blended with her own daily doings, the whole making a curious tissue of love, as fine and delicate as it is tender and true.

To turn to the brother's journal from the sister's is a fruitful lesson in human nature. In her life everything is related to him. In his she is an element, an episode, beloved, delightful, nothing more. Her name hardly occurs in his Journal, even casually. The letters he writes to her are affectionate, and appeal for comfort when he needs it. He was the sun of her life. In his, even before his marriage, she was only a tranquil star, shining quietly, treasured, but not always remembered. She knew this. Love always knows. Looking back, after he was gone, she wonders if she did not sometimes bore him. While she had him with her, the longed-for letters used to come, not always bringing what she demanded of them. "How my fingers burned to open that letter in which at last I was to see you. I have seen you, but I do not know you. You open only your head to me. It was your heart, your soul, the very inmost of your being, what makes your life, that I hoped to see."

No lack of response made any difference in the sister's ardent affection, however, unless perhaps to increase the ardor, as sometimes happens in this inconsequent world. Eugénie's thought was ever on the beloved object, on his reading, on his thinking, on his material condition, on his varied failure and success in his efforts to overcome the maddening poverty which hampered his progress. Yet how strange are the vagaries of the human heart. With all her passionate thought and affection, I do not find that she gave much heed to the one interest which was positive in Maurice's life, his desire to achieve enduring beauty for the delight of men. When a life is devoured by this longing, it measures all things and all people by their sympathy with it and contribution to it. It is perhaps just here that Eugénie failed to evoke the entire response she looked for from her brother's heart. To be sure, when his writings were gathered together after his death, she expressed great interest and some enthusiasm. Yet even then her chief anxiety was that he should not be misrepresented, misunderstood, mispraised as pagan rather than Christian, and she did not hesitate to assert that he had no thought of fame and did not desire it.

How even our most unselfish love is absorbed in its own point of view! How hard it is to love others as they would be loved, not as we would be loved. Eugénie worried perpetually about Maurice's soul, but very little about his reputation. She had not learned the profound truth and beauty of Madame de Choiseul's remark: "I have always had the vanity of those I love: that is my fashion of loving."

I wonder whether the young wife from the far Indies, whom Maurice married when death was already beginning to lay its hand on him, had any more sympathy with his aspirations for this world. There is no evidence that she had, though she was tender and devoted in her care and ministrations to the very last.

It is most curious to observe Eugénie's relation to this new sister. Even for a mother, who has her own distinct, assured claim, it is hard enough to give up a son she loves. But a sister, with all a mother's love, but only a sister's intimacy, cannot see the forming of a new and stronger bond without some dread, some repugnance, some coldness at the heart. Eugénie, like all persons who analyze their feelings, was naturally inclined to doubt others' affection because she doubted her own desert. When her friends fail to write to her, she hints her grief about it. When the tone of Maurice's letters is indifferent, or she fancies that it is, she frets and broods over it. "Do you remember that little short letter that tormented me for a fortnight?" How, then, did she bear the intrusion of a stranger heart, sure to see into all the hidden places where even she had not been privileged to come? We can divine well enough how hard it was. Her tone about her new sister might indeed seem to be all praise. She is good, she is beautiful, she is devoted to Maurice, she fulfils all her duties and is a sweet companion and friend. Nevertheless, there is the faintest, perfectly unintentional patronage. Her family are not, perhaps, quite all they should be. Her dress, charming, delightful, appropriate, but is it a little startling for a country town, that black velvet hat with an ostrich plume, fit to amaze earth and heaven, as a neighbor puts it? But we do so want to be friendly, to do our part. "I hope Maurice will be happy with her. She is n't just the sort of woman I am used to, for character, or heart, or face. She is a stranger. I am studying her. I am trying to get her near to me, to enter into her life, if she cannot enter into mine."

When they both together were soothing the last hours

of the beloved one, Eugénie has nothing but praise
and affection for her sister-in-law. But who could miss
the poignancy of the quiet remark that the sister lies
awake all night and hears the wife ministering to the
husband as she herself would like to minister? It is
hard to tell which is more significant, this comment or
that of a few weeks earlier: "They are happy. Maurice
is a perfect husband. He is worth a hundred of what
he was a year ago. He told me so himself. He confides
in me just as much as ever. We often talk together
intimately."

On one point Maurice's marriage seems to be as sat-
isfactory as it could be, that of religion. His wife does
not appear to have distracted him in any way from his
salvation, which would have been hard for Eugénie; nor
yet does the wife promote it more than the sister did,
which would have been even harder. Maurice's salvation! That was the object of Eugénie's daily thoughts
and of her nightly prayers. Maurice's salvation! While
she had him under her own motherly wing, all was well.
He might perhaps have been too easily distracted, not
intensely serious, as she was; but at least his faith was
firmly grounded and she sent him out into the great
world, confident that he would be a white soldier of
Christ always.

Alas, how often such hopes are disappointed! Not
that Maurice really sinned, or went astray. Most would
have thought him virtuous enough, Christian enough.
But he took a certain interest in the heresies of his
adored teacher, Lamennais, and, to the half-cloistered
sister at any rate, he appeared much tainted with the

follies and incredulities of an unbelieving age. How she
longed to have him back with her, at least in spirit!
How she prayed that he might pray! How she trembled
and shrank at the thought that after being separated
on earth they might not be united in heaven! "I am
not holy enough to convert you, nor strong enough to
draw you with me. God alone can do that. Oh, how I
ask it of him, for all my happiness goes with it. Perhaps
you cannot imagine, with your philosophic eye you
cannot see, the tears of a Christian eye, weeping for a
soul that may be lost, a soul so much beloved, a brother's soul, the sister of one's own."

At least she had the satisfaction of feeling that in the
end her prayers were answered and that the frail and
wavering spirit returned to die in the faith in which
she had cradled it. Taking a view with which the un-
regenerate will find it hard to sympathize, she declares
that errors of the intellect are much more serious, more
dangerous than errors of the heart. To her fond hope
it seemed that on her brother's deathbed intellectual
errors were all forgotten, and after he had left her she
resented bitterly the verdict of great writers, George
Sand and Sainte-Beuve, that he would live to posterity as a poet of nature whose essential spirit was much
less Christian than Greek.

I have said that Mademoiselle de Guérin's secluded
and in a sense impersonal life was filled by two great
preoccupations. One was her brother. It will be evident by this time that the other was God. "There is
one thing needful, to possess God," wrote Amiel at the
beginning of his Journal. Assuredly few human beings

have possessed God, have been more thoroughly possessed by the thought of God, than Eugénie de Guérin. All thoughts, all passions, all hopes, all griefs are referred constantly, in prayer and meditation, to that one source, to that one end. It is indeed beautiful to see how completely the two great interests of her life merge in each other. Madame de Sévigné adored her daughter more than God, felt and admitted that the earthly idol usurped God's place in her eager, tender, frantic mother's heart. Madame du Deffand worshipped Horace Walpole instead of God, a frail and singular substitute, it will certainly be admitted. With Mademoiselle de Guérin there was never any question of conflict. Her two loves were absolutely united, and one simply enhanced the other. To one object she addressed herself almost as freely as to the other, and it was matter of regret to her that she did not quite: "I speak as I please to this little book [her Journal, addressed to Maurice]. I tell it everything, thoughts, griefs, pleasures, feelings, everything but what can be told only to God, and even then I am sorry to leave anything at the bottom of the box."

After her brother's death, she recognizes, in a passage of wonderful self-analysis, the huge, the overmastering power of earthly affection, yet at once her permanent instinct blends God with it all in a complete, supreme effort of submission to his will. "Shall we never be rid of our affections? Neither grief, nor anguish, nor death has power to change us. To love, always to love, to love right down into the grave, to love the earthly remnants, to love the body that has borne the soul, even though the soul has fled to heaven! . . . All happiness is dead for me on earth. I have buried my heart's life. I have lost the charm of my existence. I cannot tell all that my brother was to me or how profoundly I had hidden in him all my happiness. My future, my hopes, my old age, all were one with his, and then he was a soul that understood me. He and I were two eyes in one forehead. Now we are torn apart and God has come between us. His will be done!"

In emphasizing this divine possession of Mademoiselle de Guérin, we must not, however, imply that she was actually unbalanced, or not alive to the common needs and duties of daily life. Her religion was active as well as passive. Even in the more ecstatic rites of spiritual devotion she recognizes a wholesome practical efficacy, as in her striking remark about confession. "What ease, what light, what strength come to me every time I say right out, 'I was at fault.'" Such a normal attitude makes one regret more than ever that, in our day, at any rate, those make most use of confession who have very little to confess.

In the wide practice of charity it does not appear that Mademoiselle de Guérin was especially active. Yet here too it is evident that she gave not only money but the comfort and the sage, kindly counsel which are worth much more than money, whenever occasion called for them.

So with domestic pursuits. Though her family were of old, high standing, they were poor, lived simply, kept few attendants, and the daughters of the house were wont to turn their prudent hands to every sort

of service. Eugénie had evidently been trained in the
methods of careful French housekeeping. She dusts,
she mends, she lays the table, she cooks, in emergency
she takes the linen to the brook and washes it after
the picturesque, muscular European fashion. She often
finds pleasure in all these doings, also, has a true domestic sense of order and finish and propriety. Nay, she
does her washing with real lightness of heart, seeing
charms in it which perhaps escape the average laun-
dress. "It is a real joy to wash, to see the fish swim by,
to watch the little wavelets, the twigs, the leaves, the
blossoms floating in the stream. The brook brings so
much that is pretty to the toiler who knows how to see."

But even here we note that the toiler's thoughts were
not wholly on her toil, however well she might perform
it. She was not born to labor with contented indifference. Her heart was too restless, too eager, too bent
on vast reveries beyond the limits of this world's cleanliness. Therefore she willingly lets her sister be housekeeper and only stands ready to help when needed.
If little tasks absorb too much of her time, she complains, almost petulantly. "I have hardly opened a
book to-day. My time has been passed with things
quite different from reading, things nothing in themselves, not even worth mentioning, yet which fill up
every moment." And always, through the humblest of
such tasks, runs the glowing current of those thoughts
which to her were the only reality in a world of tawdry,
trivial, incoherent phantoms. Even when the phantoms burn her fingers, she thinks only of Saint Catherine of Sienna, who had a taste for cooking. "It gave

her so many subjects for meditation. I can well believe it, if for nothing but the sight of the fire and the little burns one gets, which make one think of purgatory."

For she was thinking of hell, and purgatory, and heaven all the time, or as I said in beginning, more justly, she was thinking of God, which included them all three, and far more. God entered into every step she took, and every breath she breathed.

We may trace Him in all her earthly affections. They were deep and strong. We have seen this in regard to Maurice. It was just as true in regard to all others. Her father she cherished tenderly. She knew that he depended on her for everything and she was ready to give him everything at any moment. The deepest workings of her soul she kept from him, because she knew that he would not wholly understand them, and in covering them even with a certain duplicity she only practiced the precept of one who had penetrated the spiritual life as deeply as she, though from a different angle, "the law of love is higher than the law of truth." Her friendships for other women, also, were profoundly sincere and lasting. She gives much and asks little, just tenderness shown in a brief letter, or a fleeting word. Who has analyzed the passing of friendship more delicately than she? "It is said that women never love each other. I do not know. There may be deep affections that last only a short time. But I have always mistrusted these, for myself and for those I love. Nothing is sadder than a bit of death in the heart. Therefore, when I see an affection dying,

EUGÉNIE DE GUÉRIN

I set to work to rekindle it with all my power." Hers also is this perfect expression of a heart inclined to tenderness: "Our affections are born one of another."

Yet, as with Maurice, in all these relations God was first. The thought of Him sanctified them. The sense of his presence enhanced and beautified them. Except as they turned towards Him, they could not live and did not deserve to live. "The tenderest affections of the heart, what are they, if they are not bent towards heaven, if they are not offered up to God? They are as mortal as ourselves. We should love not for this world, but for another."

As with human love, so is it for Eugénie with all other phases of the inner life. By nature she had keen intellectual instincts, liked to read, liked to think, would even have been inclined to think with broad audacity. She had eminently the habit of reflection and analysis which makes solitude fruitful and also makes it dangerous. What scholar could express the charm of lonely hours with more depth and delicacy than this slightly tutored girl? "I love to linger over my thoughts, to bend over each one and breathe its fragrance, to enjoy them fully before they fade away." Books are a refuge, a resource, a consolation to her. She hates to leave them, even for the brief journeys she is called upon to make.

Also, the very interesting catalogue of her limited bookshelf contains some authors of distinctly profane persuasion, whom she does not always shun. Victor Hugo fascinates her. Sometimes, indeed, the quality of the text forces her to confine her attention to the pictures, but again she is wrapt by the adventures of Jean Valjean and the flamboyant mediævalism of "Notre Dame de Paris." She tries to break a long day by an exciting novel, picks "The Chamber of Poisons" for its title, but finds only disappointments, pet toads, Jesuits turned into hobgoblins, big names in petty places. She has no taste for poisons, she says. Or again, she turns to Sainte-Beuve's "Volupté," having been assured by her confessor that pure minds may pass untainted through strange regions. She likes the book, not perhaps wholly fathoming its depths of morbid suggestiveness. But the best is Molière. She tries him once, is delighted, and means to read more. Now what could be further apart than the worlds of Molière and Eugénie de Guérin?

But, in the main, she reads the writers of this life only to condemn them. Bossuet, Pascal, the Fathers, the "Imitation," are her daily and nightly company. Such books are all that Christians should read or even recognize. As for the general diffusion of book-learning and education, she deplores it with the real obscurantism of mediæval superstition. The peasants, she says, were once simple-minded, earnest, reverent, devout. Now they go to school, they read the newspapers, they acquire the superficial jargon of modern culture, and as a consequence they are atheistic in their talk and immoral in their lives.

The same intense and constant preoccupation with the mystical point of view that affected Mademoiselle de Guérin's intellectual pursuits entered into her æsthetic enjoyments. Art in its technical form was com-

pletely out of her world. She probably saw pictures
with the other curiosities of Paris, but they made no
appeal, and churches to her were churches, not in any
way creations of architectural art. Music alone she
approaches with a sort of groping sense of its vast emotional possibility. But as to this she would undoubtedly have agreed with Cowper that all music not directly intended and employed for the worship of God
was corrupting, enervating, debasing. "Oh, if I knew
music!" she cries, in a moment of enthusiasm. "They
say it is so good for the disorders of the soul." Yet it
does not touch her. "Nothing in the world has such
power to move and stimulate the soul. I know it, but
I do not feel it." And a similar experience calls forth
words profoundly characteristic for more than music.
"I listened to wonders, yet nothing astonished me. Is
there then no astonishment save in heaven?"

But there was one region of beauty in which Eugénie's soul opened and flowered with the most exquisite
delicacy and sensibility of response and that was the
world of nature. The subtle, dreamy, suggestive landscape of France, which has meant so much to poets
and painters, has rarely been felt or rendered with more
perfection than by this simple girl who spent her life
with flowers and birds and clouds and stars. "I tried
to begin a letter to you yesterday," she says, "but I
could not write. All my soul was at the window."
How often her soul was at the window, all ears, all
eyes, stirred to wild joy or grief by the breath of light
winds, or the dance of blossoms in sunshine, or the drift
of autumn leaves. Now it is fair spring weather that

delights her, now it is the long and wind-swept rains of autumn. The vast tranquillity of summer nights at times befits her mood. And again she welcomes the tumult of great storms and cries out for even thunder to jar the too monotonous quiet. Not the heart of Keats or Shelley was more vividly, more blissfully or painfully, at one with little sounds, or fleeting sights, or unknown odors that vanish as quickly as they come.

She reads Bernardin de Saint-Pierre's description of the strawberry vine, which, he says, would make matter for a volume, with all its relations and experiences. "I," she says, "am like the strawberry vine, bound up with earth and air and sky, with the birds, with so many things, visible and invisible, that I should never get through describing them, without counting what lives hidden in the folds of my heart, like the insects that dwell in the thickness of a leaf." And again, "I wish my heart did not feel the condition of the air and of the season so much that it opens and closes like a flower with cold or sun. I don't understand it, but so it is, so long as the soul is encased in this frail habitation of the body."

But nature is never all to her, never enough for her. She must have God. Either she sees Him as the whole life and beauty of it all, hears his voice in the breeze and in the storm, feels his hand in the motion of flowers and of stars, or she turns away from the beauty of earth as too apt to distract from the beauty of heaven. "The sky to-day is pale and languid like a fair face after a fever. This look of languor is full of charm. The blending of greenness and decay, of flowers that open with flowers that fall, of singing birds and creeping brooks, the breath of storm and May sunshine mingled, give an effect of fine fabrics ruffled and tossed together, of sad and sweet at once, which fills me with delight. But this is Ascension day: let us leave earth and earth's skies; let us rise above our fragile dwelling place and follow where Christ has gone before us." In another mood the quiet, subtle sounds of night seem to penetrate devotion with an overpowering tenderness, to waft thought higher even than meditation undisturbed. "It is black night. But you can still hear the crickets, the streamlet, and the nightingale, just one, which sings, sings, sings, in the thick darkness. What a perfect accompaniment to evening prayer!"

I said in beginning that Mademoiselle de Guérin had no active personal life of her own. This is as true of her as perhaps of any of us. She followed the thought of others and of God as the shadow follows the sun. At the same time, she was human, she was a woman, she was made of earth, as we all are. It is a study of exceeding interest to watch the stirrings of humanity, even barely perceptible and quickly crushed, in this white, pure vessel filled with the glow of an unearthly adoration.

Revolt she seems to have had none, doubt none, or only such momentary dimming of the pure flame as serves to make it shine the brighter. It does indeed trouble her a little to reflect that just those consolations which the poor need are given only to the rich who need them not. Life, she says, seems inside out and upside down, which was the view of Prometheus and of Satan, but in Mademoiselle de Guérin it does not strike us as Satanic. Also, her questioning of the divine order goes so far as a regret that she cannot have her doves in heaven. But this pulls her up with a shock, for in heaven we shall regret nothing — not even doves.

Some shreds of human frailty, some lingering hints of impatience and irritability and nerves, we are pleased to find that even this saint shares with us. How subtly and charmingly does she analyze them herself. "I am not in the mood to write or to do anything amiable: quite the contrary. There are days when the soul shuts itself up like a hedgehog. If you were here, how I would prick you." And again, in a little different phase. "I am most unsuccessful in dealing with difficulties, and am always in too great a hurry to get at what is to give me pleasure."

Also, I wonder whether her friends really got near her and felt at ease with her. Monsieur Anatole France speaks charmingly of *la douceur impérieuse des saintes*. Had Mademoiselle de Guérin's infinite gentleness sometimes a touch of the imperious? I can hardly prove it. It is rare and subtle and indefinable. But I divine it — a little. She remarks, with beatific triumph, "I speak to everybody I love of the things of eternity." She did. She did. And it seems merely prophetic despair to imply that the things of eternity might grow tiresome. But in this world we are contented only with eternal change.

There are some special matters of absorbing interest to most women. Eugénie de Guérin was a woman. Did she take no interest in these matters? Beauty, for instance? It does not appear that she had any special charm of feature or carriage. Was she aware of this? Did it trouble her? If so, she seldom shows it. Yet there are words here and there that set one thinking. When she was young, she says, she desired passionately to be beautiful, because she was told that if she were so, her mother would love her more. But as she grows older, she thinks only of beauty of the soul. Nevertheless, coming age seems to affect her with suggestions of ugliness, not of the soul only.

Dress again. Fair women employ it to enhance beauty, others to create it. Did Eugénie give no thought to what she should put on? Not much, I confess, beyond an exquisite sense of neatness and good order. Yet, here, too, if you watch closely, you get a gleam of human vanity, like the flash of a spangle on a sombre floor. She looks back and reviews the preoccupations of her youth, long since laid aside and forgotten, she says. "Dolls, toys, birds, butterflies I cherished, pretty and innocent fancies of childhood. Then books, talk, jewels and ornaments a little, dreams, fair dreams — but I am not writing a confession."

If she had written one, would there have been men in it, fairy lovers such as girls dream, an ideal blend of manly beauty and mad tenderness? We do not know, but here again little things make us suspect. She tells us she does not like novels, because the passions are let loose in them — but she reads them. She pities the souls in purgatory because of the terrible impatience with which they await release. What expectation on earth can compare with it? she says. Not that of fortune, or of glory, or of anything else that makes the human heart pant, unless perhaps it be the longing of the beloved waiting for the lover. And elsewhere she draws a domestic picture of quiet happiness, a little house in the fields, with vines and poultry, and some one, whom? Not a peasant, she says, like ours who beat their wives. "Do you remember —?" But she stops short and does not give the name.

In such a picture the crowning object would be children and though she does not mention them here, she does elsewhere, often, with all a born mother's tenderness. How charming is her dream of the way she would rear them and teach them. "If I had a child to bring up, how gently I would do it, how merrily, with all the care one gives a delicate flower. I would speak to them of God with words of love. I would tell them that He loves them even more than I do, that He gives them everything I give them, and besides, the air, the sun, and the flowers, that He made the sky and the beautiful stars." When Maurice's child is about to be born, after the father's death, she cries out in ecstasy. "How I long to have a baby in the house, to play mother, and nurse it, and caress it." Surely the real woman is speaking to us here.

Other feminine affairs were of less interest to her, as we have seen with things purely domestic. General society she shunned, and no doubt lost by doing so. Occasionally she is tricked out and led to a party, where she thinks every one remarks her ill, unaccustomed manner of dancing, the truth probably being that no one noticed her at all. She might, no doubt, have been successful in conversation, for she had wit, refinement, distinction, and was capable of vivacity. But she avoided what she calls the world, with a suggestion of inexpressible disdain, alleging to herself that it was futile, frivolous, and unprofitable. Perhaps a good part of the reason was that she herself was proud and shy and essentially a spiritual aristocrat. "Books are my intellectual passion; but how few there are that I like. It is just so with people. I rarely meet any one that pleases me." When you frequent the world in that spirit, it is unprofitable indeed.

One phase of human weakness did take hold of this celestial wanderer and even threaten to disturb her saintly peace, and that was the ambition of literature. She restrains it, subdues it, disclaims it. But no one could take such nice care of expression as she does, could turn sentences so daintily, so vigorously, and not take pride in them. She is like Saint François de Sales, who announces the loftiest contempt for poor words, but uses the most cunning skill to get all he can out of them.

Writing is almost a necessity to her, she says. She turns to her pen as an outlet for all the struggles and trials and passions of her inner life. "Writing is the sign that I am alive, as that of a brook is running." She looks to publication, too, makes delicate verses and sends them to a review, which she thinks will print them, if it prints women's verses at all. Not that she cares for the public, oh, no! She writes only to please a friend or two who can appreciate her. And her name must not be used in print, oh, never! Still, there is a subtle charm about this newspaper notoriety, you can hardly call it glory, which does appeal, even to the saints.

Then she thinks it appeals too much. All earthly glory is vanity, even that of the poet's corner of a magazine. Can it be right for her to spend time and thought which should belong to God on the mere tinkle of human rhyming? She consults her confessor, who assures her that no great harm is done. She consults Maurice, who is very round with her, tells her not to worry about her conscience in the matter, but to write, tells her to think a little more about the subject of her verses and less about herself, and above all suggests that she should omit devotion and mysticism and be human, advice by which he lays himself open to gentle admonition and reproof.

But she sticks to her pen just the same. Who ever failed to, that was born for it? Why, I may do good by writing, she urges. No doubt her confessor persuaded her she might, with perfect justice as regarded doing good to one person, at any rate.

But we must not emphasize too much all these petty and indifferent preoccupations. None of them really counted, none of them was more than a trifle beside the paramount, absorbing interest of Mademoiselle de Guérin's life. Not a page, hardly a paragraph, of her Journal but has some allusion to God, to her desire for God, her thirst for God, her complete, entire reference of all things earthly to what was, for her, at any rate, their origin, their purpose, and their end. She has words of marvellous mystical subtlety and grace, though the constant impression is more powerful than any single words. "When a brook runs, it starts full of foam and turmoil and grows clearer as it travels. The road I wander in is God, or a friend, but above all, God. In Him I run my course and find repose." "In this vast silence, when God only speaks to me, my soul is ravished and dead to everything else, above, below, within, without; but the rapture does not last."

Alas, no, it does not last. These ecstasies never do, whether earthly or heavenly, unless in heaven. And persons who spend their lives in waiting for them are apt to view the common, petty joys of earth with discontent. This was unquestionably the case with Mademoiselle de Guérin. A word less frequent than God in her Journal is ennui, but it is frequent enough. People bore her, society bores her, little daily duties bore her. She endures them and keeps a brave face because God bids, but the ennui is there just the same.

Nor is it only ennui. She sees a vast amount of positive evil in life. "Pessimism is half of saintliness," says an excellent authority. It was at least half of Mademoiselle de Guérin's. Besides general human suffering and cruelty and neglect, she has a set of individual troubles which seem avoidable, some doubt as to her own salvation and very considerable doubt as to the salvation of others. These things keep dark clouds over her until the sun has hard work to break through. She speaks perpetually of graves and death, always, to be sure, to draw a moral lesson from them; but cannot moral lessons be drawn from sweeter things? Even the great Christian poet, Donne, while expressing a preference for the grave, found other matters more attractive still.

> "I hate extremes, yet I had rather stay
> With graves than cradles to wear out a day."

But Mademoiselle de Guérin is more than "half in love with easeful death" and inclines to woo him with all the strange fancies of Constance in "King John." "Hippolyte talks to me of Marie, of another world, of his grief, of you, of death, of all the things I love so much."

One is inclined to break in on a strain so morbid and abnormal with reminders of "earthlier happy is the rose distilled," or with the somewhat brutal Philistinism of Horace Greeley's comment on his dear friend, Margaret Fuller, "A good husband and two or three bouncing babies would have emancipated her from a good deal of cant and nonsense."

But, though Mademoiselle de Guérin might herself have been happier as a normal wife and mother, she would not have left us the fine, elaborate analysis of an exquisite soul.

THE END